Seven Contemporary Authors

Essays on Cozzens, Miller, West, Golding, Heller, Albee, and Powers

Edited with an Introduction
by Thomas B. Whitbread

University of Texas Press, Austin and London

CONTENTS

INTRODUCTION

In this book, seven readers, all of them teachers of English at The University of Texas during 1964–1965, consider works by seven authors who could easily be their fathers, uncles, or brothers, as well as their contemporaries. Of the three authors most plausibly avuncular or paternal, James Gould Cozzens and Henry Miller are still writing, though mellower than when penning *The Last Adam* and *Tropic of Cancer* in the early 1930's, near the time their considerers were conceived and born. Nathanael West, alone, is sad and dead. No chance there for aging. And *Miss Lonelyhearts* may be the most convincingly bleak book herein discussed. Of the four authors who might be our readers' peers, two find problems of evil or inhumanity or meaninglessness located in or amid the hellish, or if not that, the human, complex fact of World War II: William Golding in *Lord of the Flies* and *Pincher Martin,* Joseph Heller in *Catch-22*. Two deal with a world recognizably postwar, while making old song, or antisong: Edward Albee in his Battle-of-the-Sexes-without-Thurber's-humor *Who's Afraid of Virginia Woolf?* and J. F. Powers in *Morte d'Urban* and shorter stories of Catholic men of God in the American 1960's.

In rereading these seven essays, originally delivered as the English Department Public Lectures for 1964–1965, I played a potentially serious game: noting all the allusions to other authors. Such a game often leads to no conclusions, is not even a *jeu d'esprit*. But here, taking into account the relative importance of each allusion in its context, the game was unusually rewarding. Among Major Influences, the Bible won over Freud by a quarter-neck. The Fall of

Man is still a little richer as a source of image and of theme than is sadomasochism to men long postlapsarian, only recently post-Freudian. The *Song of Roland* ran the Arthurian romances a dead heat. Among individual authors, those mentioned once run from Homer to John Cheever, Voltaire to Erskine Caldwell, Camus to Zola, Dante to E. A. Robinson, Juvenal to Augusta Jane Evans. Not to mention Howells, Defoe, Melville, Norman Mailer, D. H. Lawrence, Bergson, Goethe, Yeats, Mary McCarthy, Webster, C. S. Lewis, Tolstoy, and Stephen Potter. Authors mentioned twice are Faulkner, Fitzgerald, Wolfe (Thomas, not Tom), Plato, Sinclair Lewis, Saul Bellow, Joyce, Samuel Beckett, Orwell, Kafka, Shakespeare, Sartre. A list of worthies worth meditating upon! One is glad that the Avon Swan, in his 401st year, made it—much less resoundingly than Plato, but equal in that with Faulkner. But the most exciting discovery—the reward of the game—was finding three authors unique in appearing thrice. They are—this trinity—Henry James, Ernest Hemingway, Jonathan Swift.

That seven readers, writing in 1964–1965 on seven authors of works appearing from 1933 to 1964, should mention only these three other authors thrice, may seem to some a matter only for computers and their controllers. It fascinates me. For imaginatively it gets to the heart of this book. Of the three, Henry James comes off least well. R. W. Lewis, quoting a critic, puts Cozzens in a tradition of "realism" involving James, Howells, and Edith Wharton. Vance Ramsey says that *Catch-22* is "not in the Jamesian 'well-made novel' tradition." And Anthony Channell Hilfer says that such a person as Albee's George is "too disengaged from social issues to interest novelists in the Zola tradition and too empty and mannerless to interest novelists in the James tradition." Tradition, tradition, tradition. Whatever "tradition" means, James looms as a writer to be conjured with, if not dealt with. Perhaps he has been too recently overdealt with by correctors of his ignorers. Perhaps, in reaction to these correctors, he is currently underconsidered (if not underrated). Perhaps 1984 will bring him the judicious revaluation Leavis gave Keats and the middle-late Eliot gave Tennyson. According to Dr. Johnson in 1765, Shakespeare had passed the one-hundred-year test of time. Whether Henry James has such chance our essayists are chary of saying. But the fact that three of them take him as representative of a way of writing—however variously, as (1) "realistic," (2) maker of "well-made novels," (3) full-bodied and full of manners—means a good deal. It means that James wrote books of a kind seldom longer written: and of a stature against which later works, including some much like his (Cozzens'), can be measured. It may also mean that the fates of Isabel Archer, Lambert Strether, even little Maisie, are no longer felt as relevant to conditions today. Is Peter Quint at the Melopsychospiritual Clavierette irrelevant to the present of a nuclear peril no longer felt as imminently destructive, but as an unceasingly worrying buried irritant? an uncovering of sicknesses and a lancing of sores in bodies politic and psychosomatic? a world in which TV viewers can choose between local wrestling and Telstar? LBJ's latest and Danny Kaye? We shall wait and see.

Hemingway, not unsurprisingly, fares better. Mr. Lewis says that in Cozzens' *The Last Adam* "the criterion for sympathy is simply that a character earns it by operating well within his limitations—like Hemingway's heroes, performing well under pressure." Alan Friedman says Henry Miller's "*Cancer* has affinities with *A Moveable Feast*, for both truly describe, to use Hemingway's words, 'how Paris was in the early years when we were very poor and very happy'." Beautifully to kill the bull, to exalt and exult in one's twenties: what more of Hemingway? To outface nothingness. As Mr. Ramsey says, of *Catch-22*: "Life may be seen as irrational and even absurd, but beyond it looms an almost palpable nothingness, a void beyond life which is as much the experience of modern man, as expressed by Hemingway's *nada*, as is the unreason within life."

Again, Mr. Lewis: "Cozzens is Swiftian in his frequent scatological references reminding man that he is no disembodied mind . . ." A new voice, that of Roger Abrahams, who says of *Miss Lonely-*

hearts, "It is a work of utter despair, yet its ironic approach causes despair itself to be branded ridiculous . . . just as we discover that such satiric protagonists as Gulliver or Candide are the dupes of their own insular systems of thought, so Miss Lonelyhearts is revealed to be deluded by his mystical sentimentalism." And Mr. Hilfer, in his essay on Albee, says:

Our final guilt and shame, it is held in this post-Freudian era, are due to our refusal to banish falsehood and illusion about our psyches, to our insistence on rationalization and self-justification. Psychological honesty, the peeling off of labels to get down to the bare bone—this is the new ethic. This ethic might take its motto from Swift: "Last week I saw a woman *flay'd,* and you will hardly believe how much it altered her Person for the worse."

Honesty, stripping naked, seeing things to the bone plain—these are a large part of what our readers see in their authors, and in part have in common with them. But Mr. Hilfer's tone points to another important point about this volume. The writers herein do not want to be nay-sayers. They would like to affirm. They do so, in whatever ways they can.

Mr. Lewis sees Cozzens as almost the last realist, except for Saul Bellow (of *The Adventures of Augie March*). The last Adam, Dr. George Bull, "is a wonderful protagonist in his deviation from practically every expectation of a hero, particularly a doctor." And, unlike the character Herbert Banning, who can only accept and enjoy life in caring for his flowers, albeit briefly (much like Horace Benbow of *Sanctuary*), and who, "In a sense, . . . is modern man, . . . we have a Bull too, an Adam, a man who has hope, who demonstrates hope without thinking about it . . ."

Mr. Friedman says that Henry Miller, if he achieves any affirmation in his early writings, achieves "an affirmation predicated upon despair." Yet the character Henry Miller of *Tropic of Cancer* enjoys—as does Dr. George Bull—both food and sex. Food the more.

Bull, as Cozzens had it, was Adamic, and ultimately so—he had the Last Good Time in loving his life. The Miller of *Cancer* is rapt up on food, but a trifle self-conscious and romanticizing, essentially passive, about sex. In fact, as Mr. Friedman points out,

> The Miller of the *Tropics*, then, is a man who has trained himself to care for no one—and rather than run the risks of emotional involvement attendant upon normal human intercourse, he reduces all such contact to the simply sexual. Concomitantly, when every woman becomes a whore and every whore a single anatomical feature, the process, as Miller has suggested, is a lie, or rather, the poetic technique of synecdoche.

The Miller of the *Tropics*, Mr. Friedman finds finally, is "uncompromisingly bitter and self-defeating." But in the course of showing this Mr. Friedman also shows a Miller who is a lover—like Robinson Jeffers, like Brother Antoninus—of California seacoast birds.

Mr. Abrahams finds that Miss Lonelyhearts "recognizes that the basis of his malaise is his inability to fuse feeling and sense into an attitude or an effective program of action." He tries to help others. He tries to help himself. "Chaos reigns." Like author Henry Miller's character Henry Miller, Nathanael West's Miss L. is "all heart and no genitals"—essentially sexless, imitating "the sado-masochistic cycle": "sadistic action, masochistic docility, and retreat to bed and isolation." Here we have androgyny, come to ruin. Would that Miss L. were one of the 778 characters in Dickens' *Bleak House!* or a Charles Addams cartoon.

George Clark, in considering William Golding's novels of character-enlightenment, is very good on *Lord of the Flies*, superb on *Pincher Martin*. Teeth and eating are crucial to Chris (Pincher) Martin's experience—an experience centrally purgatorial. Teeth crunch, grind, smash, articulate: "On the rock, as Chris's consciously controlled memories and thoughts contemplate the stuff of the involuntary replays of his past, he first articulates the philosophy which has shaped his life and his view of life; it is a philosophy of eating—'eating women, eating men, crunching up Alfred, that other girl, that boy . . ." The past, replayed. Ego in emphasis!

Mr. Ramsey finely describes how Joseph Heller's concern for life—"What else *is* there?"—gets dramatized in his mad-sane, ferocio-comic book. Captain John Yossarian is willing to be the victim of anything *but* circumstance (in contrast to the determinism Mr. Lewis detects in *The Last Adam*). Yossarian is a true antihero, exemplifying the sane absurd: a combination of laughter with horror. The book *Catch-22* faces, and avoids, the void. At the same time, "modern evil exists" in such men as Colonel Cathcart, Colonel Kern, and, finally, Scheisskopf, "not in any overpowering, demonic guise, but in the guise of Horatio Alger dutifully climbing to success over the bleeding forms of his fellows." But individuality and assertiveness are values: like George Bull, "The positive elements in the novel which are convincing are connected with the first three-quarters in which characters live and live vitally in the teeth of almost insuperable odds for death and anonymity."

Mr. Hilfer says, "George and Martha's chant of 'Who's Afraid of Virginia Woolf' is a childish defiance of the principles of order, judgment, taste, and decency in the everyday conduct of the private life." Albee's adults seem to be naughty children playing games. The man-woman war is "love-hatred." Mr. Hilfer, near the beginning of an illuminating comparison of *Who's Afraid of Virginia Woolf* with Eugene O'Neill's *A Long Day's Journey into Night*, calls both "drama[s] of erosion," and sees in both the "wearing effect of the passage of time" literally dramatized through the "sheer pile-driving sustained repetition of verbal violence." Albee, in Hilfer's view, is "a brilliant comedian of sickness, a virtuoso of humiliation and cruelty."

Robert G. Twombly finds that J. F. Powers' Father Urban, somewhat like Pincher Martin, is obsessively self-concerned: "Urban is watching himself unceasingly in the mirrors of his own mind, watching himself critically, but without humor. This, by the way, is his sin, if he has one." And Urban's dousing in the lake is an instance, Mr. Twombly asserts, of "antisymbolism," perhaps in part like Yossarian's antiheroism. The essence of Powers' view of the problem, for too many of us, of how to get along in the world of the U.S.A., A.D. 1965, is capsuled by Mr. Twombly: "The final culprit in this book is neither a man nor a sin. On the contrary, it is the futility of moral endeavor in a world in which the only virtues are triviality and folly, and the only sins are prudence, tact, and worldly success."

The writers of these essays believe the human being has a future. They interpret his future possibilities in contexts posed by writers immediately, and not so immediately, past. As you will find, there is much humor—sardonic, open, careful, careless, shaggy-dog—in their prose.

What strikes me most strongly, though, is that all our readers, with one exception, find their authors *ironic*. The one exception is Mr. Hilfer, whose Albee falls into invective. But the six others find wry, comic, or sardonic detachment, some irony, or even paradox, in vision or style, in the authors of whom they write.

R. W. Lewis:

Bull doesn't see life in dualistic terms. For him, life *is*: nothing is real but reality, and reality is what you see around you every day. Certainly ideas are not real, and he has escaped them and is "free," as May Tupping and Herbert Banning are not. But what is Bull's free world but an enslaving deterministic one in which he can do little more than *accept* his role? To this question, Cozzens can only bring an ironic style that detaches him from commitment to any dogmatism but does not preclude sympathies with both Christianity and positivism.

Alan Friedman:

There are . . . enough [whores] in *Cancer* and *Capricorn* to people a street of brothels—and with a comic detachment, a saving irony of vision which is one of the outstanding features of Miller's writing, he records them all—the fat whores and the lean whores, the immoral and the amoral, the predatory, buzzardlike whores who are fundamentally man-haters and the merely hungry ones who, with both belly and bed warm and full, care nothing at all for a man's money.

Roger D. Abrahams: *Miss Lonelyhearts*

utilizes a totally ironic perspective while telling a story of a very real moral dilemma in psychologically realistic terms, thereby forcing the reader to sympathize with the title character and to laugh at him at the same time.

George Clark: in *Pincher Martin,* a

representation of Chris as a man who sees himself as Odysseus but whose story follows the shape of the misfortunes of Aias, the knucklehead who doomed himself by his own folly, illustrates the *irony* in Golding's conception of his protagonist.

Vance Ramsey:

The detractors of *Catch-22* have usually regarded it as disorderly mixture of comedy, satire, farce, and invective; the book's admirers, on the other hand, have stressed the basic seriousness and purpose beneath the apparently disorganized and purposeless surface.

The ironic humor of *Catch-22*, as Ramsey says, is that of the "picaresque epic" and the "anguished farce" combined: "mortality returns like a theme in music, each time with variations of meaning, but each time essentially the same." One of the themes is that of having been "disappeared":

Throughout the book men are "disappeared," a chillingly apt term. Dunbar, Clevinger, Major Major—in one way or another all seem to die or disappear. The terms of life or death, existence or nonexistence, are irrational and arbitrary. Mudd, a man who was to have lived in Yossarian's tent but who was killed before he reported for duty, is alive administratively because to admit his death would be sloppy bookkeeping. Doc Daneeka, on the other hand, is administratively dead and spends the rest of his time forlornly trying to assert his existence.

Robert G. Twombly displays the narrator in J. F. Powers' *Morte d'Urban* as ironic, as are the symbols of Urban's wetting and emersion. Then:

Father Urban, here at the end of the novel, is quite free of the taint of pride. And from the disappearance of the ironic narrator some reviewers infer that the spirit of moral criticism has come to rest.

This fading out of the ironic narrator at the end, interestingly, is the only way in which Powers can convey a change in attitude within his central character.

And then, with fine awareness, about "Powers' only truly moving story, 'Lions, Hearts, and Leaping Does' ":

Father Didymus is an old man who has watched himself kill one affection after another, ostensibly for his religion, but actually (as he knows too well) through nothing better than the disease of alienation that afflicts ironic and cynical men. He let his brother die unvisited, and knows now that the reason was not an attachment to a higher love, but simply the cynic's acquired detachment from all loves of any kind.

Much is in common among these authors, among these readers. Most in common, in its various modes, is the ironic stance. How better confront *nada*? or a past or passing sure hierarchical vision? or even, paradoxically, that supreme ironist, Swift, himself? two hundred and more years dead? All flesh is as the grass. All flesh is flesh.

Thomas B. Whitbread
The University of Texas, Austin

The Conflicts of Reality:
Cozzens' **The Last Adam**

R. W. Lewis

Some reasons for discussing a less-than-popular novel are that it is a neglected masterpiece, a forgotten classic, or a forerunner of some vital movement. James Gould Cozzens' *The Last Adam* is none of these things—neither wholly neglected nor forgotten, nor a forerunner of anything except more Cozzens novels. But it is a very skillfully *patterned* novel; it is a good introduction to Cozzens because it foreshadows many of his later themes and techniques; it is relatively short compared to other later novels of his—a pedagogic advantage; it deals with a recurrent theme in American literature, that of the American as Adam; and it is an interesting and entertaining novel in its own right. For these reasons I propose to examine some of its outstanding features and some problems in the novel and how they are solved.

Cozzens the man is of no particular interest here, nor is the slowly growing body of scholarship on his work. Very little is to be said about his life, that began in 1903, because very little is known. The depth of this ignorance is attested by the fact that a *Time* magazine cover story is still the best source of intimate information about Cozzens' life. Although there are now nine volumes in the Cozzens canon (Cozzens himself having chosen to omit his first four novels as "apprentice work"), Cozzens was pretty widely unknown until *By Love Possessed* made the best-seller lists and ultimately set off a critical controversy in 1957 and 1958. Even winning the Pulitzer Prize with *Guard of Honor* in 1949 (the novel was published in 1948) had won him but the scantest attention, and that not initially from the heavyweight critics but from Stanley Edgar Hyman, Bernard DeVoto, and Granville Hicks.[1] Two sound and also sympa-

[1] See, for instance, the total silence with which Edmund Wilson (*The Shores of Light* [New York: Farrar, Straus & Young, 1952] and *Classics and Commercials*

thetic essays in the fifties by Frederick Bracher and Louis O. Coxe
gave some promise of elevating Cozzens into the ranks of his contemporaries who had arrived—if only in survey courses in the modern
American novel. And then his properly developing career and
reputation were given fame's kiss of death. *By Love Possessed* was
called "a masterpiece," "Tolstoyan in size and seriousness."[2] Brendan Gill, Malcolm Cowley, Jessamyn West, and Granville Hicks
gave the novel high praise in their reviews, and John Fischer (in
Harper's) nominated it for the Nobel Prize. Some of these reviewers also charged that "the critics" had shamefully neglected Cozzens, but Cozzens actually had always been widely and regularly
reviewed.

The reaction of another group of critics was inevitable, and Cozzens, unfortunately, was caught in the crossfire. "The critics" defended themselves from the first reviewers by attacking Cozzens.
And the novel at hand—*By Love Possessed*—couldn't quite stand
the hostile scrutiny. The sympathetic reviewers had done Cozzens'
reputation no favor, but for all that, the hermitic author gave no
sign of caring, and the recent, thus far muted appearance of a new
volume, *Children and Others* (1964), published at Cozzens' lei-
surely spaced rate seven years later, seems evidence that he works
on while critics like Irving Howe make fun and Lana Turner makes
the Hollywood version. Cozzens' literary reputation has apparently
withstood the assaults of inconstant fame; among critics, the success
of a contemporary author is always suspect, but Cozzens has been
validated as a serious author by a continuation of scholarly articles
about his work, the special number of a journal devoted to him,[3] a

---

[New York: Farrar, Straus, 1950]), Alfred Kazin (*On Native Grounds* [New
York: Reynal & Hitchcock, 1942] and *Contemporaries* [Boston: Little, Brown &
Co., 1962]), and Frederick J. Hoffman (*The Modern Novel in America* [Chicago:
Henry Regnery Company, Gateway Editions, 1956]) regard Cozzens.

[2] Brendan Gill, "Summa cum Laude," *The New Yorker*, 33 (August 24, 1957),
98, 100.

[3] *Critique*, 1 (Winter, 1958).

review of research and criticism about him,[4] and five books on his work, three now published and two promised, one of which is a full descriptive bibliography.[5] In short, Cozzens doesn't need apology, and anyone dealing with the history of the modern American novel must henceforth deal with him.

Perhaps a close reading of *The Last Adam* will indicate that this dealing, at the very least, will be a pleasant task with considerable intellectual stimulation. Cozzens is a novelist outside the mainstream of the modern American novel because of some of his attitudes and techniques, but still very much an *American* novelist who writes novels more distinctly American in their themes and characters than much of the popular egocentric American fiction that is American only in the technicality of its settings. As Harry John Mooney, Jr., has put it, "Cozzens is in many ways the prototype of the *impersonal* writer."[6] If he is out of the mainstream of the contemporary American novel, he is at least in the tradition of Henry James, William Dean Howells, and Edith Wharton, the American tradition of realism, or, to use Richard Chase's distinction, "the tradition of the novel as opposed to the romance, which is free from the novel's requirements of verisimilitude, development, and continuity." The romance tends "towards melodrama and idyl," and has "a more or less formal abstractness and . . . a tendency to plunge into the underside of consciousness." And most importantly in contrast to Cozzens' work, the romance has "a willingness to abandon moral questions or to ignore the spectacle of man in society, or to

---

[4] Richard M. Ludwig, *Texas Studies in Literature and Language*, 1 (Spring, 1959), 123–136.

[5] Frederick Bracher, *The Novels of James Gould Cozzens* (New York: Harcourt, Brace & Co., 1959); Harry John Mooney, Jr., *James Gould Cozzens: Novelist of Intellect* (Pittsburgh: University of Pittsburgh Press, 1963); D. E. S. Maxwell, *Cozzens* (Edinburgh: Oliver & Boyd, 1964). John Lydenberg has announced a book in progress, and Richard M. Ludwig and James B. Meriwether are working on the bibliography.

[6] Mooney, *Cozzens: Novelist of Intellect*, p. 2.

consider these things only indirectly or abstractly."[7] Cozzens is a rationalist and in a sense a classicist who is very much concerned with man in society. Contrasted with the intensities of Faulkner, Wolfe, Fitzgerald, and Hemingway, Cozzens is dispassionate and detached though far from indifferent to the fates of his characters or their society. Beginning with *The Last Adam* in 1933, he has written novels about the morals and manners of cross sections of American life, and he has had doctors, ministers, lawyers, and Army officers as his protagonists, not adolescents (usually tortured), bootleggers (usually in star-crossed love), or Southern families (usually depraved). Of course, Life with a capital L has all these people in it, and American literature is stimulating not only because of the great number of good American writers but also because of their varying techniques. The literature is enriched by this diversity; and only a reader with very limited tastes would neglect one or the other kind of writing. Intrinsically, New England doctors are just as interesting novelistic materials as depraved Southern families, and instead of worrying over rankings and Pulitzer Prizes and making odious and useless comparisons, we ought to be happy in the differing but very real pleasures of such a novel as *The Last Adam*.

In this novel Cozzens' method is essentially that of his later, longer novels, and in a letter to his English publisher, he described what he wanted to do in *Guard of Honor*. His remarks apply also to *The Last Adam:*

What I wanted to write about here, the essence of the thing to be said, the point of it all, what I felt to be the important meaning of this particular human experience, was its immensity and its immense complexity. . . . I could see I faced a tough technical problem. I wanted to show . . . the peculiar effects of the interaction of innumerable individuals functioning in ways at once determined by and determining the functioning of innumerable others—all in the common and in every case nearly helpless involvement in what had ceased to be just an "organi-

---

[7] Richard Chase, *The American Novel and Its Tradition* (Garden City, New York: Doubleday & Co., 1957), p. ix.

zation" . . . and become if not an organism with life and purposes of its own, at least an entity, like a crowd. . . . I would just have to write off as readers everyone who could not or would not meet heavy demands on his attention and intelligence, the imagination to grasp a large pattern and the wit to see the relation which I could not stop to spell out between this & that.[8]

Let me underscore several points in this letter: Cozzens does not abstract from experience but tries to convey large bodies of experience in all their complexity; life as he sees it is an immensely complex interweaving of the actions and reactions of every person within a given setting; life is patterned and the realistic novel is patterned, but the unsimplified presentation of the patterning demands an attentive reader who will see the importance of a missing horseshoe nail to the fictive kingdom that Cozzens rules.

In *The Last Adam* these patterns take the form of conflicts that seem to subsume a dualistic universe. As a result of unseasonably mild and rainy February weather in a small Connecticut town, the water reservoir is contaminated, and the pollution brings on a typhoid epidemic. The sole doctor in town, sixty-seven–year–old George Bull, diagnoses the typhoid fever as spring fever, for which he blithely passes out castor oil. Then he resumes his pleasantly animal life, that includes an earthy but well-born mistress, robust drinking and eating, a snake hunt, and ironic baiting of virtually everyone in town, but especially the wealthy and powerful few who run the town. Doctor Bull changes his diagnosis (at the prompting of his ancient Aunt Myra) and works hard inoculating the healthy and tending the sick and dying. His enemies seize this moment when public opinion is aroused against him to demand his resignation as county health officer. The town Democrat (equivalent to the village atheist in Midwestern towns) speaks in Bull's defense at the town meeting, and the same sort of chaos that brought on the epidemic and its repercussions saves the doctor's job and

---

[8] Quoted in Bracher, *The Novels of Cozzens*, pp. 67–68.

something of his reputation (which, of course, he doesn't give a hoot for).

Some obvious oppositions or conflicts in this action are between sickness and health; life and death; the haves and the have-nots; the sensualists and the puritans; the free, adventuring bodies and minds and the paralyzed, tradition- and society-bound bodies and minds; the moral, the immoral, and the amoral; and reality and some mental construct or dream of what should be real. These conflicts are successfully dramatized through contrasting settings and characters and, in a rather more sophisticated way, through a roving narrator's point of view, that lets the reader see successive scenes through the eyes of a wide range of characters, including not only many of the major characters but also some of the minor ones. The action covers a relatively brief period of twenty-six days in a deliberately limited setting of a New England town, but the effect is that of a "big" novel, in part because we not only meet a lot of characters but also see parts of the action through their eyes. And all of them are remarkably individualistic even when they are of minor importance. Cozzens creates a Connecticut microcosm, and the multiplicity of characterization tends to heighten the theme of conflict and even chaos. The esthetic irony, of course, is that the artist conveys confusion through the order of his art, and Cozzens seems to be saying that beneath this superficial multiplicity and confusion is a single social organism that absorbs all these characters and reconciles all their seeming antagonisms.

Throughout this novel run ambiguities, dilemmas, and tensions —as between theory and practice, the ideal and the real, lust and love, or, as in the title of another of his novels, the just and the unjust. In *The Last Adam*, for instance, Doctor Verney, the up-to-date young doctor who cares for the wealthy Banning family, has an impressive array of degrees, nurses, laboratory facilities, and medical theories. George Bull has never used the secondhand microscope he bought long ago in the hope that it might some day be useful; he is totally without a bedside manner, and, more importantly, he is a thoroughgoing determinist who holds little stock in medicine as an efficacious science: with typhoid, at least, it really doesn't matter much what the doctor does, for a certain percentage of the stricken will die, a certain percentage will recover. With the two doctors thus representing two theories of medicine, Cozzens contributes one pair of opposites to the larger thematic pattern of conflicts. Louis O. Coxe has also noted this pattern throughout Cozzens' work, and he describes it as the double vision of modern man, the central paradox of action and contemplation, of understanding and conduct, of the ironic view and the heroic view.[9] Cozzens' intelligence will not allow him to subscribe to any dogma, whether it is social, political, or religious; his humaneness, on the other hand, will not allow him or his sympathetic characters to resign themselves to overwhelming fate, to endorse in one way or another anarchy or chaos. Man's condition is limited by his environment and by his own nature, that seems to be made up of the forces of reason and passion—the white horses and the black horses. Whatever the reality of man's nature, Cozzens says that man must recognize and accept his limitations and still "operate," just as the waiter in Hemingway's "A Clean, Well-Lighted Place" operates in the quiet bravery of his resistance to an encroaching nada. In Cozzens, the resistance may be that of the well-named Doctor Bull who opposes the incongruities and contradictions of life with an unreflecting vitality that delights in action and the pleasures of the flesh. (The English title of the novel was, incidentally, *A Cure of Flesh*.) Another form of resistance or an attitude that will enable one to function in such a complex world, however, is reflective and here is best illustrated by May Tupping, who isn't able to realize most of Bull's delights because her husband is almost totally paralyzed and she is poor. In trying to find satisfactory answers to the reason why she couldn't go to college and later why fate saw fit to cripple her husband in a freak hunting accident, she has read widely in the New Winton library, including

[9] Louis O. Coxe, "The Complex World of James Gould Cozzens," *American Literature*, 27 (May, 1955), 157–171.

"the thirty-odd volumes containing all that was best in the world's literature," books that seemed "at least a godsend" to her.[10] But Cozzens' god is a jester, and May never finds ultimate answers, though she is, at least, entertained. What are the great philosophies of the world if they cannot tell her why the snobbish "Bannings should be rich, while Mrs. Talbot was destitute," or why her husband Joe was shot and not his companion Harry Weems? Plato, she decides, has nothing to do with "the realities of existence.... [Plato's philosophy] was pure wisdom, untouched by common sense."

Left to herself, and to what she could see of the universe, real and ideal were lost together in an indifference so colossal, so utterly indifferent, that there was no defining it. This immense mindlessness knew no reasons, had no schemes; there was no cause for it. Where could it begin, and why should it end? There was even an error in personifying the universe as It, saying: How could It either plan or prevent Mrs. Talbot's misfortunes? How could It care? "Only, I care," May thought. "I think it's terrible. It oughtn't to be that way." (210)

In considering the mutual influences of existentialism and literature, Professor Bernhard Blume has found existential heroes under every kind of bush.[11] Perhaps May Tupping is another one. In any case, her circumstances and temperament have denied her the vitalness of a Doctor Bull, and she is not content to accept paradoxes and inconclusive positions. She does raise a meek voice of protest; she stands out from all the other characters in her humility and her attempt to oppose the void with a consciously induced but sincere kindness in the face of great odds. It is true that Cozzens makes us laugh at her naïveté and prudishness, but she is altogether a sympathetic figure. And her loving kindness ultimately works as well as Bull's vitality, for she alone among the major characters benefits

---

[10] James Gould Cozzens, *The Last Adam* (New York: Harcourt, Brace & Co., 1933), p. 209. References in this paper will hereafter be in the text itself, and all references will be to the Harvest Books edition, New York, n.d.

[11] "Existentialism and Literature," a lecture given at The University of Texas, Austin, October 29, 1964.

from the typhoid epidemic: by some curious chemical fate, her husband Joe's paralysis is cured when he gets a mild case of typhoid fever. One might hold such a happy solution suspect, but May doesn't feel she has "learned" anything from the partial evil that is total good for her. In fact, her good fortune combines the heroic and ironic views of life: virtue is rewarded but the agency is mindless, accidental fate. One cannot feel any sort of triumph.

May is something of a Job figure, and Biblical allusions and quotations abound in the novel. Doctor Bull is the last Adam; he is in no paradise, but he is unconcerned with the problems of being that concern May and a number of the other characters. Herbert Banning and Matthew Herring are not afflicted as Job and May are, but they too have a keen sense of what *ought* to be. Wealthy and respected, they nonetheless are uncomfortable in spirit when they are faced with problems such as how to treat their servants (in a supposedly democratic society) and how to keep Doctor Bull in his place or even get revenge on him (in a supposedly Christian society). One other most interesting minor character, Justice of the Peace Henry Harris, has something of Bull's cavalier contempt for ideas, but he is inconsistent for he does desire fame and power. About all other matters he is cynical, but it is he who defends Bull when the Bannings and their ilk go after Bull's job and reputation. Partially, he is serving his own interests, of course, but he defends Bull's mistakes with fine irony because he argues on truly Christian grounds. The mob hypocritically subscribes to Christianity, but it is the village cynic who saves Bull. After his speech, Matthew Herring tells him,

"Henry, you're quite a speaker! You've beaten me. But I don't think you can beat truth and decency. Not every time, at any rate."

"Why, Matthew," Henry Harris answered, turning his delighted grin from Miss Kimball and her notebook. "I never have any quarrel with intangibles." (301)

At the beginning of the novel May is reading in *Pilgrim's Progress* of Christian's triumph over death, but at poor Mamie Talbot's burial young Virginia Banning thinks the prayers are absurd:

Mamie, stretched out, shut up in the shrouded coffin, would probably think that they were making fun of her. As it is to the wise, a word to the weak is sufficient. Unless you were proud, strong, well up in life, you had no need to be reminded at such length that you were nothing and went down like grass. Who could doubt it? (147)

Bull roars out "Adeste Fideles" when he is taking a bath; his frequent hymn singing and his memory of some verses from Job are merely a residue of his education as the son of a minister. Right after telling May that Joe is recovering he heads for his mistress' house and on the way pauses to study the night sky: "George Bull stood a moment regarding it, for Boötes was one constellation he could remember. Mechanically he said: 'Canst thou bring forth Mazzaroth in his season? or canst thou guide Arcturus with his sons?' God, by his mighty works, convinceth Job of ignorance, and of imbecility!" His father had taught him "to recognize the eternal stars recommended to Job," but now "he could see well enough what bad sense and worse logic the old man had once terrified him into considering wisdom" (259–260). Science is the only truth, the only faith worth believing in, and yet when it comes to looking for aid, science in the form of modern medicine is little more help to man than religion ever was. Some of the townspeople "get down on" Doctor Bull when he is absent at Mamie Talbot's death, but there would have been nothing that he could have done.

The real trouble was I forgot to put on a big show entitled "The Wonders of Science." . . . When I was first practicing, they kind of thought a doctor was a medicine man. They didn't know what it was all about; he was sort of dabbling in the occult, and anything he did was all right with them. They don't know any more now; but they've been reading the papers and they want some of that, not God knows what out of a bottle. You ought to see Verney's place. Nurses sitting around in uniform making urinalyses. Half a ton of fluoroscopic machines. Verney telling

all the women to get undressed for a thorough examination. When he's
through, he has a four-page record. Nine cases out of ten, he doesn't
know a thing he couldn't have found out by feeling a pulse and asking
a couple of questions. Talk about the occult! (180–181)

Later, after the typhoid has struck, Bull and Dr. Verney work hard,
but Bull has little faith in whatever they do. He tells his mistress
Janet Cardmaker that the mortality rate of virulent typhoid fever
is about 17 per cent. Since the town has forty-three or forty-four
cases, it is "perfectly certain" that seven or eight will die. Facts are
facts. But there is some adventure in wondering who the seven or
eight will be.

Probably eighty out of a hundred typhoid cases will get well without
any treatment or cold baths or nonsense. At least fifteen will die any-
way. That means you might have five to fool with. If you don't happen to
kill them [as Bull admitted that he once had killed a boy with appen-
dicitis] perhaps you'll cure them. Verney was showing me all the figures. Huh! It's funny what a point of view does for you. An old horse
doctor like me looks at them and all he can see is that medical science is
perfectly useless in ninety-five out of every hundred cases. When Verney
sees them, he finds the other five show how wonderful whatever tricks
happen to be in style are. (260–262)

It would be wrong, however, to assume that all of Bull's views are
also those of the author Cozzens. And we do learn in Henry Harris'
defense of Bull at the town meeting that the vital statistics of the
state "prove" that Bull has been a good doctor and county health officer: in twenty years New Winton was never ranked poorer than
tenth out of 169 Connecticut towns. Bull, of course, would be the
first to deny the relevance of the figures to a test of his competence,
but facts are facts to the townspeople, and they go away satisfied
while the shrewd Yankee trader Harris, the irreverent and fatalistic
Bull, and Dame Fortune all enjoy a good laugh.

But Harris, it will be remembered, is doing something more than
seizing the day as Bull is; Harris wants power and fame. Bull is a

wonderful protagonist in his deviation from practically every expectation of a hero, particularly a doctor. Sinclair Lewis seemed to
hold the scientist in awe, and his medical scientist Martin Arrow-
smith comes the closest of his protagonists to a heroic figure, but
Cozzens' doctor exemplifies a mighty peculiar list of heroic qualities: he is an agnostic, a determinist, a hedonist—or perhaps better,
a vitalist, an aristocrat who thinks it is a tremendous joke that his
fellow aristocrat Janet Cardmaker is a sensualist who has so little
reverence for their colonial past that she sells her antique furniture
and even the stairway of her old family home to a New York Jew;
he is also a pragmatic moralist—a polite phrase for a hypocrite and
bigot who bullies other people but is incensed when an enemy (the
father of the boy he killed) slashes his tires while he is visiting his
mistress; he also mocks Catholics and immigrant Poles, and his
mistress' description of him as an "old bastard" would seem, out of
context, something of an understatement. Yet Bull is heroic, and the
secret of his bullish stature is his vital Adamic quality. That Cozzens
calls him the *last* Adam is in part an indication that his later novels
will not have such heroes: they will have, rather, protagonists who
incline to be rational compromisers—mature, responsible, disci-
plined, slightly older and wiser male counterparts of May Tupping.
A rather more interesting but frightening reading of Bull as the
last Adam is the suggestion that our world breeds no more original
creatures who are their own masters, thirsty and hungry for pleasure, contemptuous of the past and the future, strong, independent,
even arrogant, bold, self-contained, and vital, the very "antithesis
of the 'social' man," shrewd rather than intelligent and free of the
neurotic doubts or guilt feelings that cripple Herbert Banning and
make of him, for all his good mind, good heart, and good family, a
womanly figure who putters around in his garden and can only
react rather than act.[12] Another understanding of how "last" is
meant by Cozzens is revealed at the very end of the novel; Bull's

[12] Bracher, *The Novels of Cozzens*, pp. 26 and 37.

Adamic qualities are indestructible; they will last to the last: Janet thinks of him as he rests in her kitchen:

> There was an immortality about him, she thought; her regard fixed and critical. Something unkillable. Something here when the first man walked erect; here now. The last man would twitch with it when the earth expired. A good greedy vitality, surely the very vitality of the world and the flesh, it survived all blunders and injuries, all attacks and misfortunes, never quite fed full. She shook her head a little, the smile half derisive in contemptuous affection. Her lips parted enough to say: "The old bastard!" (314)

Frederick Bracher thinks Cozzens is guilty of "sentimental primitivism" and that he is *praising* Bull,[13] but I read his characterization as well-balanced, sympathetic certainly, but not without the qualifications that are dramatized by Bull's contrasts with other sympathetic characters such as May Tupping and even Virginia Banning, whom Bull himself admires and who has no "greedy vitality" at all: she is one of those who dies in the epidemic. Cozzens'—or any realistic novelist's—best characters are alive because they are complex and at times contradictory.[14] As a doctor, Bull tends to think of people as animals, which he is himself in his animal-like stretching and grunting and eating and making uncomplicated love, as well as in his name. But he—and Cozzens—know that man thinks in a way that other animals do not; when Bull himself is tired—that is, when his vitality is reduced—he too is contemplative and melancholy. Cozzens is Swiftian in his frequent scatological references reminding man that he is no disembodied mind; but Cozzens is also something of an intellect who writes in an allusive style, and in this novel May Tupping is something of an intellectual, and a sympathetic one. In this diversity among characters as well as complexity within characters, the criterion for sympathy is simply that a char-

---

[13] *Ibid.*, p. 46.
[14] See Richard M. Ludwig, *Princeton University Library Chronicle* (Autumn, 1957), p. 7, and Bracher, *The Novels of Cozzens*, p. 103, who quotes Cozzens on "such unresolved paradoxes of personality."

acter earns it by operating well within his limitations—like Hemingway's heroes, performing well under pressure.

Cozzens is also saying that the oppositions or conflicts are superficial or even artificial, but perhaps man needs a false dualism—as between good and evil, wealth and poverty—to help him make sense out of life. The "best" life either avoids the extremes or simply ignores them while still keeping a tension between the functional but purely abstract poles. For a reflective person like May Tupping or Herbert Banning, the conflicts are very real in so far as they exist in their "real" minds and seem to shape their very vision of the world. But Bull demonstrates that such a vision is not the only one, and he functions very well without it. Bull doesn't see life in dualistic terms. For him, life *is*: nothing is real but reality, and reality is what you see around you every day. Certainly ideas are not real, and he has escaped them and is "free," as May Tupping and Herbert Banning are not. But what is Bull's free world but an enslaving deterministic environment in which he can do little more than *accept* his role? To this question Cozzens can only bring an ironic style that detaches him from commitment to any dogmatism but does not preclude sympathies with both Christianity and positivism.

Cozzens' brand of determinism is more thoroughgoing than that of most modern American novelists. Or perhaps it is simply that in this novel determinism is more centrally pertinent than it is in other contemporary novels where determinism is an assumption of the novelist and not a point that needs discussion. At least, Cozzens generates tremendous ironies in depicting New Winton's citizens as so many puppets moving to and fro on a stage as if they knew what they were doing but really being manipulated by the invisible wires of heredity and environment. Of course a few of these puppets are paradoxically or painfully sentient. Although Bull is a creature of appetite, he probably had to do *some* thinking to get his M.D., and he is sardonically amused by the mass of people whom he sees as more controlled than controlling: for instance, "Belle Rogers was one of a locally recurring pale, wan, blond type, descended probably

from a single pale, wan, but prolific individual five or six genera-
tions back" (34). Janet's father with his "little round head," and
"aimless, vaguely human activity suggested one thing only" when
in his senility he held his book upside down and hung his arms
loose: "Mr. Cardmaker was an ape. The only important dissimi-
larities would be his relative hairlessness and inefficient teeth" (37).
True, man aspires, and gets college degrees, but he is caught up in
the whirl of a social organism that most men can neither understand nor control. Herbert Banning, so unlike Dr. Bull in many
ways, is like him in seeing the relative futility of his own actions
and desires.

The very setting of the novel reinforces the feeling of tension or
irresolution. The time of the novel spans one month from the last
week in February to the third week in March, when the weather is
erratic and fluctuates between cold snowy days and warm pleasant
ones. And Cozzens makes the most of the weather imagery: at the
very end of the novel, when the time is closest to spring, the faithful,
hopeful May Tupping looks out on a new snowfall and thinks, "This
was like winter beginning all over again; but she felt strong enough
to stand it; for sooner or later it had to be spring; and Joe would be
well" (312–313). As mentioned before, Doctor Bull diagnoses typhoid fever as spring fever when there is a sudden break in the
winter weather at the end of February. In the central episode in the
novel, the burial of Mamie Talbot, the townspeople agree that the
mild weather cannot last: "Most people said that they had never
seen anything like it. By Friday, this spring in the midst of winter
became as natural as life in the midst of death. Sunday would be
the first day of March; and once it was March, a mere change of
name could change what was wrong and amazing for February into
what was right for spring" (155). It is even hard to accept a dualism
of life and death, and a doctor especially would be aware of their
unity; from the moment of birth he has watched many of New
Winton's citizens dying; the very life-giving mothers are themselves always aging, coming nearer death. And one of the many

deaths in the novel is that of Sal Peters, who dies in an abortion. The robust 215-pound Doctor Bull contrasts with the skinny Mamie Talbot and Virginia Banning—flat-chested, thin-skinned, hollow-cheeked—who are among those who can't fight sickness. Some men are leg-men, some men are bust-men, but Cozzens is a bone-man, and he has both Bull and May Tupping seeing the skull and the skeleton beneath the flesh: "The big bones of [Janet Cardmaker's] face made her look gaunt, but she was, in fact, very solid; stronger than most men . . ." (32). Janet's dying cow that Bull examines (he thinks of himself as a horse doctor) has a bony head and protruding ribs. Janet's dead father had a "skin-covered face without flesh" (37). A blush stains, not Virginia Banning's cheeks, but her cheek-bones. Doctor Bull consumes gargantuan breakfasts, but Virginia Banning has only a cup of coffee, and her brother thinks of her as starving and becoming a "living skeleton" (96–97). She is in rebellion against her genteel family, and for her fierce independence, Bull admires her. But she is suicidal in her reluctance to nourish the flesh that Bull so delights in, and in a brilliantly descriptive passage she comes close to killing herself in a maniacal compulsive ride in her brother's high-powered automobile. Typhoid is only the agent of her self-inflicted death; her nurse looks at her "narrow buttocks," "her narrow chest" and "those piteous flat breasts." "There was no flesh to sustain her" (309–310), and as she is dying "her very bones itched through her flesh" (149).[15] She really has had something of a death wish, for only through death could she have the freedom of a man like Bull. Ironically, at the very time she becomes ill, her parents decide to let her go on a long trip, and now she wants to live. But fate is indifferent, and death claims her as readily as it had claimed Virginia's counterpart, the Bannings' poor skinny servant Mamie Talbot, who is the same age as Virginia. Some of the towns-people accuse Mrs. Banning of working poor Mamie to death; the

---

[15] See also May Tupping's view of Mamie Talbot's wasted body, pp. 99–100.

Banning sympathizers accuse Doctor Bull of neglecting her. But the truth is that heredity and environment did her in.

Thus while there are some ironic parallels between Mamie and Virginia, they both contrast with Doctor Bull, and nowhere is he better seen in symbolic action than in the snake-hunting episode. When Janet Cardmaker calls Bull an old bastard, she unwittingly alludes to Adam, who had no earthly father. (Bull's real father, appropriately enough, was a minister of God.) During the warm weather, Doctor Bull, Harry Weems, and Lester Dunn climb a ridge outside of town to kill rattlesnakes, and it is then that Bull unequivocally performs as a modern Adam seeking vengeance on the snake responsible for his loss of paradise: Bull leaps on the heads of the rattlers with his heavy hobnailed boots, partly fulfilling the prophecy of Genesis that Adam shall bruise the snake's head and the snake shall bruise Adam's heel. Here, however, a snake bites Doctor Bull on the thumb, and, in addition to the Biblical allusion, another pertinent one, and an ironical one, is to the snake of Asclepius, a symbol of renovation and of the doctor's curative powers. But while the episode is interestingly allusive, it seems somewhat intrusive, since it is not central to the action, as are the other episodes. Just as it is a diversion for Doctor Bull to go snake hunting, so is the episode a mere decorative addition to the plot.

In general, however, Cozzens is artful in the interweaving of his episodes into the single pattern that through character, image, symbol, and theme as well as action demonstrates the complex, conflicting nature of Cozzens' vision of reality. Between Bull and the Bannings, Henry Harris and Matthew Herring, Virginia Banning and Guy Banning, antitheses wax and wane. The very seasons of spring and winter struggle against each other; sickness and health, life and death, wealth and poverty oppose and mingle; freedom and vitality are obtained and demonstrated through a wide spectrum from Bull's nearly complete self-mastery to the social enslavement of Herbert Banning, the physical paralysis of Joe Tupping, the professional

narrow-mindedness of Doctor Verney, and the mental bankruptcy
of Mrs. Talbot; in respect to vitality, the bull-like persons oppose
the sluggish snakes, still benumbed by some metaphysical cold just
as the rattlers are in the cool early spring weather—Mrs. Banning
and Joel Parry try to trick Doctor Bull, and in doing so they are
hypocritical; vitality is further illustrated in the characters' use and
abuse of sex: to Guy Banning it is some-thing to do with some-body
on a weekend college party, and it is as casual as smoking the pipe
he has affected because too many of the wrong people have taken
up cigarette smoking; to some of the townspeople adultery is the
only kind of adventure left for them in their otherwise dull, drab
lives; for bulls like the doctor and Janet's huge Jersey bull named
Moloch (after a Semitic deity who, like the doctor, was worshipped
through the sacrifice of children) sex is a vast animal pleasure that
is creative rather than destructive and personal rather than dehumanized and mechanical. This mechanized sex is symbolized in the
sexually allusive, mad automobile ride that Virginia Banning takes
and that ends so close to the literal death that she avoids with her
legs locked together; other cars and trains too suggest the sleek
mechanized impersonal sex of Guy Banning's and Donald Maxwell's—the village satyr's—sort. Doctor Verney's thorough stain-
less-steel-and-test-tube brand of medicine is also felt by Virginia
Banning to be a kind of violation; and certainly the power line
whose construction leads to the epidemic has symbolic suggestions
of another kind of doom for lovely women who stoop to folly. But
Doctor Bull's relation with Janet is certainly without sentimentality
or mechanization, and it is virtually without emotion; Bull is happy
with her because he is free to enjoy and he has nothing to pretend.

One other machine or instrument should be noted, not because
it is relevant to the treatment of sex but because it completes the
pattern of oppositions that are mechanically symbolized; to May
Tupping (who serves as a kind of chorus) time is of great importance because time takes care of everything in her sorrow-filled
life: you knew the dentist would hurt you in your afternoon ap-

pointment, she thinks, but by five o'clock, it would all be over; and death was something that passing time took care of too. In her job as telephone operator, she listens in on the life and death communications of her world, and she watches the bank clock, waiting for the hour when her period of duty will be done. But the precise, mechanical regulation of her life is artificial, and it contrasts sharply with Doctor Bull's irregular wanderings. Perhaps May thinks that time will take care of her and Joe's suffering just as it finally did Mamie Talbot's, but time has nothing to do with Joe's providential recovery. Another means of measuring time is the sundial in Herbert Banning's garden: it is not a machine but an ingenious and old device that his mother had placed in the garden, not for telling time but as a memento mori: "You were to think how little time remained to prepare to face your Maker, not how little time remained in which to be happy." Around the old dial plate is inscribed: "It is later than you think" (304). The Puritan past rises up to haunt Banning; he is without his mother's faith, he is full of self-doubts and agonies, he does not want to but he does frustrate his rebellious daughter Virginia, and all he can do is play at being the country squire. *His* sense of time has made him impotent too, and he is unhappy even before his daughter dies; life is *supposed* to be different, he avers. Who but an animal would do nothing but accept it?

Herbert Banning is wealthy and powerful, well-educated and well-born, but he is caught in dilemmas and indecisions and conflicts and tensions that will not be resolved except by death. The only acceptance of life that is his is in caring for his flowers, and he cannot enjoy even that activity very long without the intrusion of painful thought. In a sense, he is modern man, but *here*, Cozzens is saying, we have a Bull too, an Adam, a man who has hope, who demonstrates hope without thinking about it as May Tupping does. "The last Adam," as Cozzens' Biblical source says, "is a life-giving spirit."[16] Doctor Bull is not the American as Laocoön wrapped

[16] I Corinthians, 15: 45.

round in the despairs that stifle Banning, so aptly and negatively named. As R. W. B. Lewis says in *The American Adam*, neither view of mankind is complete in itself, but in this present age of crisis and containment rather than commitment and hope, our fiction— Cozzens' later novels included—has tended to lose sight of the reality of spontaneity and vitality, of the legitimacy of action even when it is absurd, of delight in nature even if it is incomprehensible.[17] Recent American fiction does have other Adams, like Saul Bellow's Augie March, but they have begun to re-emerge only recently to carry the literary battle to their despairing fellow protagonists who have for too long been holding the field, and in their hopelessness presenting a world view as innocent and naïve as that of Billy Budd or Jay Gatsby. It is perhaps the chief distinction of Cozzens' novel that he so successfully dramatizes a microcosm in which both kinds of heroes are fully and fairly drawn.

[17] "Epilogue: The Contemporary Situation. Adam as Hero in the Age of Containment" (Chicago: The University of Chicago Press, 1955).

The Pitching of Love's Mansion in the **Tropics** of Henry Miller

Alan Friedman

More than any other year, 1926 climaxed the era of the so-called "Lost Generation" of American expatriate writers, although by then almost all their important documents, from Sherwood Anderson's *Winesburg, Ohio* in 1919 to F. Scott Fitzgerald's *The Great Gatsby* in 1925, had already been written, published, and received. The year 1926 was climactic, however, since that year was Hemingway's—it was the year of *The Sun Also Rises* and it was the last of the *Moveable Feast* years—and Hemingway, despite his subsequent repudiation of Gertrude Stein's "dirty, easy labels,"[1] has come to epitomize the writers of his era, the writers we still glibly label "the Lost Generation."

Henry Miller, in 1926, was still in America, though he was *of* America far less than any of his self-exiled compatriots; for with the exception of the very early years, when he was growing up in Brooklyn, and the late years, when he was settled in his Big Sur Paradise, Miller has been consistently vehement in his opposition to everything he sees America symbolizing. "I can think of no street in America," he writes in *Tropic of Capricorn*,

or of people inhabiting such a street, capable of leading one on toward the discovery of the self. I have walked the streets in many countries of the world but nowhere have I felt so degraded and humiliated as in America. I think of all the streets in America combined as forming a huge cesspool, a cesspool of the spirit in which everything is sucked down and drained away. . . . Over this cesspool the spirit of work weaves a magic wand, palaces and factories spring up side by side, and munition plants and chemical works and steel mills and sanatoriums and prisons and insane asylums. The whole continent is a nightmare pro-

---

[1] Ernest Hemingway, *A Moveable Feast: Sketches of the Author's Life in Paris in the Twenties* (New York: Charles Scribner's Sons, 1964), p. 31.

ducing the greatest misery of the greatest number. I was one, a single
entity in the midst of the greatest jamboree of wealth and happiness
(statistical wealth, statistical happiness) but I never met a man who
was truly wealthy or truly happy.[2]

And elsewhere he expresses his fears of America's influence on
the entire world: "I see America spreading disaster," he writes, "I
see America as a black curse upon the world. I see a long night
settling in and that mushroom which has poisoned the world with-
ering at the roots."[3]

But by 1926 Miller had yet to discover Paris, the Paris where,
as he puts it, he was to be "born and reborn over and over. Born
while walking the streets, born while sitting in a cafe, born while
lying over a whore. Born and reborn again and again" (*Black
Spring*, p. 161). In 1926 Miller was not only still in America, still
unknown and still spiritually isolated, but he was already thirty-
five—nearly a decade older than Hemingway—and he was just
beginning to write full time. Up to this point he had written, in
addition to a series of prose-poems he attempted to sell from door
to door, a single still-unpublished novel, and he was to produce two
more before his fourth, *Tropic of Cancer*, was finally published, in
Paris, in 1934.

Thus, although for the next quarter of a century he remained a
kind of writer non grata in England and America, Miller the artist
and Miller the cause had been simultaneously born, and born, it
should be noted, to the sound of trumpets and a hallelujah chorus.
Here, for instance, is Lawrence Durrell, one of the many early
hymnists, hailing *Tropic of Cancer*:

It strikes me as being the only really man-size piece of work which the
century can really boast of. It's a howling triumph from the word go;
and not only is it a literary and artistic smack on the bell for everyone,

---

[2] Henry Miller, *Tropic of Capricorn* (New York: Grove Press, Inc., 1961), p.
12; hereafter *Capricorn*.

[3] Henry Miller, *Black Spring* (New York: Grove Press, Inc., 1963), p. 21; hereafter cited in the text.

but it really gets down on paper the blood and bowels of our time. I
have never read anything like it. I did not imagine anything like it
could be written; and yet, curiously, reading it I seemed to recognise
it as something which I knew we were all ready for. The space was all
cleared for it. *Tropic* turns the corner into a new life which has regained
its bowels. In the face of it eulogy becomes platitude. . . . I love its guts.
I love to see the canons of oblique and pretty emotion mopped up; to
see every whim-wham and bagatelle of your contemporaries from Eliot
to Joyce dunged under. God give us young men the guts to plant the
daisies on top and finish the job.[4]

Granted, Durrell was only twenty-two at the time, and might not
be expected to know any better, but, with almost undeviating consistency, such self-indulgent hyperbole has characterized his view
of Miller ever since—and it has become an increasingly typical
attitude as more and more voices have blended in an uncritical hailing of Miller's supreme significance.

But if Miller enthusiasts have tended to view him as a cause, as a
banner around which they could rally in eager defiance of all the
authoritarian taboos they glibly associate with Anglo-Saxon society, at least they have not gone the way of his equally vehement
detractors who completely ignored the artist for the cause. For instance, according to Elmer Gertz, the trial lawyer who successfully
defended *Tropic of Cancer* in Chicago, the self-righteous California
judges who had earlier ruled Miller's two *Tropic* books obscene,
"presumed to pass upon the character, or the morals, of Miller, the
unorthodox ideas that outraged them, his sexual explicitness, and
the use of four-letter words of Anglo-Saxon origin, and they gave
little credence to the literary experts who held the *Tropic* books in
high esteem."[5] In writing of the landmark Chicago trial of *Cancer*,

---

[4] Lawrence Durrell, in Lawrence Durrell and Henry Miller, *A Private Correspondence*, ed. George Wickes (New York: E. P. Dutton & Co., Inc., 1963),
p. 4.
[5] Elmer Gertz, "Henry Miller and the Law," in *Henry Miller and the Critics*,
ed. George Wickes (Carbondale: Southern Illinois University Press, 1963), p.
181; hereafter *Critics*.

Hoke Norris has noted that time and again either hearsay or a quick glance at a page or two of the book was enough for the self-appointed guardians of community morality. "This sort of instantaneous literary and judicial judgment," he writes, "is to be found throughout the case, not only among police officials but also among some newspaper columnists, clergymen, and the writers of wrathful letters."[6]

Norris goes on to cite various police actions against the book, as well as statements by the police chiefs involved; the following case is typical. One captain, the acting chief of a Chicago suburb, was asked if he believed he was enforcing the state obscenity law when, without a warrant and on his own initiative, he pressured local booksellers into removing *Tropic of Cancer* from their shelves. " 'No, I wouldn't say the state law,' replied Captain Morris. 'We were just enforcing a moral law which I believe has a place in a town such as ours where we have good, religious people and many churches'."[7] The full implications of such a statement are truly frightening to contemplate.

For many of us in the English-speaking world, then, the name Henry Miller conjures up thoughts of a more or less noble crusade against proper Bostonians and their ilk throughout the land; for, despite the hopes of Miller and his many fervent supporters, he has gained a reputation in his native country based not primarily on widespread recognition of his uncommon genius, but rather on his ability to rouse the shocked sensibilities of some and the civil libertarianism of others. The censorship war, of course, has been going on at least since the time of Plato, who feared the influence of the poets on his young Guardians, and it seems likely to continue a good while longer. In 1933, in response to Judge Woolsey's now historic decision on Joyce's *Ulysses*, Morris Ernst wrote that "the *Ulysses* case marks a turning point. It is a body-blow for the

---

[6] Hoke Norris, " 'Cancer' in Chicago," reprinted from *Evergreen Review*, No. 25, p. 5.

[7] *Ibid.*, p. 8.

censors. The necessity of hypocrisy and circumlocution in literature has been eliminated. Writers need no longer seek refuge in euphemisms. They may describe basic human functions without fear of the law. . . . Under the *Ulysses* case it should henceforth be impossible for the censors legally to sustain an attack against any book of artistic integrity, no matter how frank and forthright it may be. We have travelled a long way from the days of Bowdler and Mrs. Grundy and Comstock. We may well rejoice over the result."[8] Unfortunately, in the afterglow of victory, Ernst mistook a single battle for the entire war—a war in which we have since witnessed the battles of *Lady Chatterley's Lover*, of *Fanny Hill*, of *Tropic of Cancer*, a war, in fact, which is far from ended. The Marquis de Sade, to mention only the most obvious, still looms in the future, as does perhaps a third of Miller's published writings.

One must assume, especially considering the many remarkable opinions written by various courts in the last few years, that the war is being won—and it need detain us no further. Still, it does warrant our consideration since Miller the cause—a Miller obviously noble, obviously on the side of the angels—tends to become inextricable from Miller the artist, a figure of still questionable stature. Stanley Kauffmann, in one of the most balanced reviews of *Cancer*, focuses on just this problem in considering the inflated praise the book has evoked. "I hazard a couple of guesses at extrinsic reasons for this," he writes. "First, when a gifted man writes a prosecutable book, it is often over-lauded as a tactical move by those interested in the freedom of letters—especially those who hold that sex is Beautiful, not sexy. Second, possibly these statements are, as much as anything else, a tribute to Miller's purity of commitment, to his abhorrence of the pietisms of Literature and the proprieties of the Literary Life, to his willingness—if not downright eagerness—to suffer for the right to live and write as he chooses. His is no small

[8] Morris L. Ernst, "Foreword" to *Ulysses*, by James Joyce (New York: The Modern Library, 1946), pp. vii–viii.

spirit," Kauffmann concludes, "it is just not as large as some have told us."[9]

Let us, then, examine that spirit Miller offers us in his early fiction, *Tropic of Cancer*, *Black Spring*, and *Tropic of Capricorn*, focusing primarily on *Cancer*, the first, most important, and best of this loosely connected trilogy. Two prefatory points should be made before continuing, however. First, it should be noted that Miller is extremely difficult to quote in brief, for what most characterizes his writing—and represents both the best and the worst thing about it—is his interminable jamming together of formless, exuberant imagery. Miller, in fact, writes like a Spasmodic poet, seemingly afraid that words are going out of style and, unless he employs them all immediately, they will be lost to us forever.

Second is the question of whether these books are novels at all. Miller insists they are not, even to the point where he writes an outraged response to a highly favorable article by Edmund Wilson simply because the latter had assumed that *Cancer* is a work of fiction.

Wilson praised Miller for his skilful ironic portrait of a particular kind of "vaporing" poseur, for making his hero really live, "and not merely in his vaporings or his poses. He gives us the genuine American bum come to lead the beautiful life in Paris; and he lays him away forever in his dope of Pernod and dreams." To all of this praise for irony, Miller replied:[10]

The theme of the book, moreover, is not at all what Mr. Wilson describes: the theme is myself, and the narrator, or the hero, as [Wilson] puts it, is also myself. . . . the narrator . . . is me, because I have painstakingly indicated throughout the book that the hero is myself. I don't use "heroes," incidentally, nor do I write novels. I am the hero, and the book is myself.[11]

[9] Stanley Kauffmann, "An Old Shocker Comes Home," in *Critics*, p. 159.
[10] Wayne C. Booth, *The Rhetoric of Fiction* (Chicago and London: The University of Chicago Press, 1961), p. 367.
[11] Henry Miller, in a letter to *The New Republic*, May 18, 1938, reprinted in *Critics*, p. 29.

Wayne Booth, in his brilliant study of the novel, cites this exchange between Wilson and Miller as exemplifying the contemporary critic's dilemma when considering the crucial question of distance between author and character, and he sympathizes with Wilson for making a very natural error. But there is overwhelming evidence that, despite Miller's protestations to the contrary, Wilson is basically right and Booth wrong. In *Cancer*, for instance, the protagonist writes that "I have made a silent compact with myself not to change a line of what I write. I am not interested in perfecting my thoughts, nor my actions."[12] And yet the first draft manuscript of *Cancer* was three times the length of the published version, and three times Miller rewrote the book.[13] With regard to his Chronology, a supposedly factual account of his life, Miller has said: " 'Here and there I'm deliberately putting down a lie—just to throw the bastards off the track'."[14]

The same, of course, goes for his "autobiographical romances," as he calls them—only more so. For instance, after vividly detailing an extensive series of sexual conquests, the protagonist of *Capricorn* says: "It was going on this way all the time even though every word I say is a lie" (190). Samuel Beckett, in a perhaps apocryphal story, was asked if the title character of *Waiting for Godot* was meant to be God. "Of course not," he supposedly answered, "if I had meant God I would have said God; I meant Godot." Whether

[12] Henry Miller, *Tropic of Cancer* (Paris: Obelisk Press, 1960), p. 20; hereafter *Cancer*.

[13] See, for example, the "Chronology," by Miller, for the year 1934, printed in *The Best of Henry Miller*, ed. Lawrence Durrell (London, Melbourne, and Toronto: Wm. Heinemann Ltd., 1960), p. 385; hereafter *Best*. On p. 37 of the same book, Miller writes that *Cancer* "was written several times and in many places —in Paris." Durrell tells us that *Cancer* "was distilled out of a colossal MS which I was lucky enough to read, and which could not have been less than fifteen hundred pages long. It seemed to me that there was enough material to make three or four *Tropic of Cancers* from it" ("Studies in Genius: Henry Miller," in *Critics*, p. 105).

[14] Quoted by Lawrence Durrell in *Art and Outrage: A Correspondence about Henry Miller*, by Alfred Perles, Lawrence Durrell, and Henry Miller (London: Putnam & Co., Ltd., 1959), p. 55.

the incident actually occurred is beside the point; its moral remains loud, clear, and relevant: be wary when an artist speaks of what he intended by his work. Perhaps it would be best if, as E. M. Forster suggested, we read all literature as though it were written in a single huge room, simultaneously and in effect, anonymously. In practice, however, we need to strive for a satisfactory mean between the two extremes, especially when, as in Miller's case, author and protagonist have identical names and largely coextensive lives. As Kingsley Widmer, in the best book to date on Miller, had noted, "it is unavoidable in discussing Miller's work to call the central figure Henry Miller, as does Henry Miller, though this is not a claim that the experiences are literal fact. . . . in all probability Miller's writings about Miller are not true, in several senses."[15]

These early books, then, with their loosely connected, anecdotal narrative, deal primarily with an alienated aging American writer who divides his thoughts and energies between the intoxicating life of Paris and the frenzied life of New York, and who discovers that the world is essentially an uncongenial place for such sensitive, personable individuals as himself. *Cancer's* similarities with *The Sun Also Rises* have been noted many times, as for instance in this comment by Samuel Putnam, a cohort of Miller's in the early Paris days and also a minor character in *Cancer*: ". . . whatever may be said of Miller, he has summed up for us as no one else has the expatriates' Paris of the second phase: and I think it may be said that the *Tropic of Cancer* is to that phase what *The Sun Also Rises* is to the preceding one."[16] In addition, *Cancer* has affinities with *A Moveable Feast*, for both truly describe, to use Hemingway's words, "how Paris was in the early days when we were very poor and very happy."[17] For even though hungry, Hemingway tells us, the young, eager, in love, expatriate writer of the 1920's found Paris "a move-

[15] Kingsley Widmer, *Henry Miller* (New York: Twayne Publishers, Inc., 1963), p. 8.
[16] Samuel Putnam, "Henry Miller in Montparnasse," in *Critics*, p. 15.
[17] Hemingway, *A Moveable Feast*, p. 211.

able feast." But by the time of *Cancer* the hopeful twenties have given way to the forlorn thirties, and the prototype of the hungry writer has become a middle-aged lecher making nihilistic gestures at all the old romantic shibboleths. And thus the causes of Miller's happiness are more complex and more obscure than Hemingway's, for the latter is young and the work is going well and he is generally satisfied with the world he inhabits. If in *his* early writings, Miller ultimately achieves an affirmation of sorts, it is an affirmation predicated upon despair, for one by one he has rejected all the traditional values, all the consolations conceived by other men and other artists. The very point of *Cancer*, in fact, as Mark Schorer has put it, "is that he has divested himself of every connection and responsibility in order to be free to do nothing but live with no money, no obligations, no residence, nothing except himself for life, and at that point he says, 'I am the happiest man in the world'."[18]

This world, Miller insists, is a cancerous zone, a hospital full of the dying and the deadly: "People are like lice," he says—"they get under your skin and bury themselves there. You scratch and scratch until the blood comes, but you can't get permanently de-loused. Everywhere I go people are making a mess of their lives. Everyone has his private tragedy. It's in the blood now—misfortune, ennui, grief, suicide. The atmosphere is saturated with disaster, frustration, futility" (21). And out of this misery his imagination thus imposes upon others, emerges a perverse kind of drunken glee, for "the effect upon me," he claims, "is exhilarating. Instead of being discouraged, or depressed, I enjoy it. I am crying for more and more disasters, for bigger calamities, for grander failures. I want the whole world to be out of whack, I want everyone to scratch himself to death" (21). What Miller means, apparently, is that his spiritual malaise finds solace, even delight, in an external despair at least as negative as the one within.

In addition, *Tropic of Cancer* reads as a kind of scatological *Down*

---

[18] Mark Schorer, testifying in the case of "Commonwealth of Massachusetts vs. *Tropic of Cancer*," printed in *Critics*, p. 162.

and Out in Paris and London, for like the Orwell book, it concerns
the quest for food and shelter (among other things) during the days
and nights of the Parisian Depression—only Orwell seeks even the
most menial and degrading work in order to survive at any cost;
Miller, on the other hand, becomes a parasite in order both to survive on his own terms (that is, without working) and, despite his
protestations to the contrary, in order to make literature of the experience. At the beginning of *Cancer*, Miller offers us a miniature
portrait of the artist and his art.

It is now the fall of my second year in Paris. I was sent here for a reason
I have not yet been able to fathom. I have no money, no resources, no
hopes. I am the happiest man alive. A year ago, six months ago, I
thought that I was an artist. I no longer think about it, I *am*. Everything
that was literature has fallen from me. There are no more books to be
written, thank God. This then? This is not a book. This is libel, slander,
defamation of character. This is not a book in the ordinary sense of the
word. No, this is a prolonged insult, a gob of spit in the face of Art, a
kick in the pants to God, Man, Destiny, Time, Love, Beauty . . . what
you will. I am going to sing for you, a little off key perhaps, but I will
sing. (11–12)

Art, then, becomes non-art, for it is not only formless and eclectic,
negative and destructive, but it serves for the artist not as an end in
itself but as a means to life. Elsewhere Miller writes that "art is only
a stepping-stone to reality. It is the vestibule in which we undergo
the rites of initiation. Man's task is to make of himself a work of art.
The creations which man makes manifest have no validity in themselves; they serve to awaken." Consequently, he concludes, the
artist must cease "immolating himself in his work," must cease
creating out of a martyrdom "of sweat and agony. . . . We do not
think of sweat and tears in connection with the universe; we think
of joy and light, and above all of play."[19] And this is the kind of nay-
saying which, since it is ultimately affirmative, we can readily ac-

[19] Henry Miller, "Of Art and the Future," from *Sunday After the War*, reprinted in *Best*, p. 237.

cept—for even if art is not simply a spontaneously formed out-
pouring, even if art is not simply unrecollected and untranquilized
emotion, it is pretty to talk as if it were.

Of Miller's semiautobiographical fiction, there are, to date, a total
of nine excessively large volumes. They are unified primarily by
similarities of mood and atmosphere, and only secondarily by subject matter, by, for instance, the dual theme of loss of innocence
and initiation into manhood—an initiation which Miller's picaro
has undergone enough times to become a fraternity unto himself.
From time to time he renders this theme explicit, as when he dis-
cusses the effect upon himself of Henri Bergson's book, *Creative
Evolution*: "When I think of the book now, and the way I approached it, I think of a man going through the rites of initiation.
The disorientation and reorientation which comes with the initiation into any mystery is the most wonderful experience which it is
possible to have" (*Capricorn*, p. 220). Nonetheless, and despite the
rather earthy form such initiation usually takes in these writings,
Miller's central concern in them "was not with sex . . . but with
the problem of self-liberation."[20] Richard Ellmann, in testimony
given during the Chicago trial of *Cancer*, expressed essentially the
same view of that book when he said that " 'there is nothing which
is attractive about sexuality as represented in it'." Very much unlike, for example, *Fanny Hill*, a book which exalts sex, joyfully
delighting in it and the life devoted to it, *Cancer* is rather " 'a criticism of life in Paris at that time and, by extension, a criticism of
life throughout the world at that time'."[21]

Miller's focal theme, and he expounds it at lengths sometimes
painfully graphic, sometimes enormously funny, is disgust and
revulsion at the stupidity and ugliness he sees all about him—and
because his disgust and revulsion are both profoundly felt and often
ineffectually transmuted into art, and because disease must, after

---

[20] Henry Miller, in *The World of Sex*, reprinted in *Best*, p. 356. Miller is
speaking specifically of *Cancer*, but the same holds for his other fiction.
[21] Richard Ellmann, quoted in " 'Cancer' in Chicago," pp. 14, 12.

all, be represented by disease, Miller rages on like a tidal wave of sewerage:

If there were a man who dared to say all that he thought of this world, there would not be left him a square foot of ground to stand on. When a man appears the world bears down on him and breaks his back. There are always too many rotten pillars left standing, too much festering humanity for man to bloom. The superstructure is a lie and the foundation is a huge quaking fear. If at intervals of centuries there does appear a man with a desperate hungry look in his eye, a man who would turn the world upside down in order to create a new race, the love that he brings to the world is turned to bile and he becomes a scourge. . . . If any man ever dared to translate all that is in his heart, to put down what is really his experience, what is truly his truth, I think then the world would go to smash, that it would be blown to smithereens and no god, no accident, no will could ever again assemble the pieces. (240– 241)

And because Miller would be this man and because he is a frustrated romantic whose vision of reality bears virtually no resemblance to the stagnant world he sees about him, his naïveté and his disillusionment give way, at times, to strident nihilism and profound despair. "I can't get it out of my mind," he says in *Cancer,* "what a discrepancy there is between ideas and living" (235). Nonetheless, the romanticism, the wide-eyed wonder of youthful innocence, not only clings but at times breaks forth into lyric passages of perhaps surprising beauty, as in the following passage from *Big Sur,* a much later book by a much mellower Miller:

There were always birds: the pirates and scavengers of the blue as well as the migratory variety. (At intervals the condor passed, huge as an ocean liner.) Gay in plumage, their beaks were hard and cruel. They strung out across the horizon like arrows tied to an invisible string. In close they seemed content to dart, dip, swoop, careen. Some followed the cliffs and breakers, others sought the canyons, the gold-crested hills, the marble-topped peaks. . . . From the ocean depths there issued strange formations, contours unique and seductive. As if the Titans of the deep had labored for aeons to shape and mold the earth. Even millennia ago the great land birds were startled by the abrupt aspect of these risen shapes.[22]

Even as early as *Cancer,* however, the lyrical Miller is not only present, but present when we might least expect him. Perhaps despite himself, his bubbling enthusiasm for life, for all of life, is self-infectious, and he continually breaks out in a hives-like joyfulness. Having written, "we're all dead, or dying, or about to die," he almost immediately refers to himself as "incurably optimistic! Still have one foot in the 19th century. I'm a bit retarded, like most Americans. . . . The mere thought of a meal—*another* meal—rejuvenates me. A meal! That means something to go on—a few solid hours of work, an erection possibly. I don't deny it. I have health, good, solid, animal health. The only thing that stands between me and a future is a meal, *another* meal" (46, 55).

Food, in fact becomes *Cancer's* one transcending standard of value. Art may be an intrusion, love a diseased prostitute, and the world a rotting corpse, but food, that divine inspiration, is God's glory on earth. "Food," Miller writes with gusto, "is one of the things I enjoy tremendously" (13). And perhaps it is the only thing he enjoys tremendously always, for Miller, who often seems obsessed with the fact that he is not Jewish, adopts the traditionally Jewish belief in the therapeutic powers of food, in food as a nostrum for all the ills of life. Upon his long-delayed return to his parents' home in Brooklyn, a guilt-ridden Miller writes elsewhere, he feels a sudden compassion for the lower-middle-class sterility of their lives. But then, after the tears of this necessarily temporary reunion have been shed, the family turns, as usual, to the inevitable next meal. "The table was set; we were to eat in a few moments. It seemed natural that it should be thus, though I hadn't the slightest desire to eat. In the past the great emotional scenes which I had wit-

[22] Henry Miller, *Big Sur and the Oranges of Hieronymus Bosch* (New York: New Directions, 1957), p. 7.

nessed in the bosom of the family were nearly always associated with the table. We pass easily from sorrow to gluttony."[23]

The problem in *Cancer*, however, is far less likely to be that of gluttony than that of hunger. At one point, Miller's hunger becomes so acute that, despite his essentially passive, nonassertive nature, he feels constrained to initiate corrective action. Realizing "that no one would refuse a man a meal if only he had the courage to demand it," he writes to a dozen or so acquaintances, asking each the day of the week it would be convenient to have him come to dinner. Not only do none refuse him, but even those who can't stand him wine and dine him royally. "They were all obviously relieved," he writes, "when they realized that they would see me only once a week. And they were still more relieved when I said—'it won't be necessary any more.' They never asked why. They congratulated me, and that was all. Often the reason was I had found a better host; I could afford to scratch off the ones who were a pain in the ass" (60). Miller, for his part, never thinks to ask why his hosts do give him up so readily, but it is apparent that his feelings for them were mutual. Miller, however, continues blithely on. " 'Life,' he quotes Emerson as having said, 'consists in what a man is thinking all day.' If that be so," he adds, "then my life is nothing but a big intestine. I not only think about food all day, but I dream about it at night" (73).

But Miller's dreams and fantasies are as much sexual as they are gastronomical, and Paris serves equally well as caterer and procurer. "I have never seen a place like Paris," Miller comments, "for varieties of sexual provender" (160). And for the picaro of *Cancer*, life in Paris becomes, as much as anything else, an attempt to sample as much as possible of this so generously provided provender. The whorey hordes, like marching Chinamen four abreast, parade incessantly down the streets of Miller's cities—streets he associates, both literally and figuratively, with life in the raw and, therefore,

[23] Henry Miller, "Reunion in Brooklyn," from *Sunday After the War*, reprinted in *Best*, p. 99.

with life unclothed in the devitalizing, dehumanizing raiments worn by everyone who is not of the streets. As Miller puts it in *Black Spring*: "What is not in the open street is false, derived, that is to say, *literature*." And he adds, "I was born in the street and raised in the street. . . . To be born in the street means to wander all your life, to be free" (1–3).

And thus Miller seeks out his whores, creatures of the street par excellence, and romanticizes them as fellow free spirits: Tania, with her "fat, heavy garters," her "soft, bulging thighs," "a Tania like a big seed, who scatters pollen everywhere," a Tania who is the loveliest Jew of them all, and for whose sake, Miller exclaims, "I too would become a Jew" (*Cancer*, pp. 13–15); Germaine, who bore all the obvious signs of her way of life (the boozy breath, the cheap jewelry, the rundown heels, the pasty rouge accentuating what it was meant to conceal), and yet like Molly Bloom exhibits in bed such an earthy joyousness—a joyousness clinically or cynically called nymphomania—that Miller quite naturally finds her delightful; and Claude, who, unlike Germaine, was not really cut out for this line of work, who was, at bottom, "just a good French girl of average breed and intelligence whom life had tricked somehow," and who "had a soul and a conscience . . . [and] refinement, too, which is bad—in a whore," and whom for a while Miller thought he loved (51).

There are, of course, innumerable others—enough in *Cancer* and *Capricorn* to people a street of brothels—and with a comic detachment, a saving irony of vision which is one of the outstanding features of Miller's writing, he records them all—the fat whores and the lean whores, the immoral and the amoral, the predatory, buzzardlike whores who are fundamentally man-haters and the merely hungry ones who, with both belly and bed warm and full, care nothing at all for a man's money. And because, like Yeats's ultrarational Crazy Jane, Miller can never forget that love has pitched its mansion in the place of excrement, his amatory encounters read like a series of experimental investigations into the accuracy of her assertion. Necessarily, Miller emphasizes those human organs, traditionally unmentionable and even at times unthinkable, which serve dual functions for Crazy Jane—and for everyone else. The duality is central when Carl, for whom Miller has been ghost-writing love letters for six months, at last goes to meet his rich, widowed correspondent. Although the lady is not only willing but downright eager, the luckless Carl spends the entire evening unable to find a delicate way of telling her that his bladder is full to bursting.

Later on in *Cancer*, when Miller gives us a description of Carl's room, he notes that "in the *bidet* were orange peels and the remnants of a ham sandwich" (277). The convenient and, in France, omnipresent *bidet* is, of course, the perfect symbol of the dual functioning of the sex organ, and Miller makes good use of it, as when he rails at Claude's offensive delicacy. "Who wants a *delicate* whore!" he demands. "Claude would even ask you to turn your face away when she squatted over the *bidet*! All wrong! A man, when he's burning up with passion, wants to see things; he wants to see *everything*, even how they make water" (53).

The *bidet* also plays a key role subsequently when in a typical surrealistic flight of fancy, Miller imaginatively abstracts from his picaresque narrative and arrives at an existential epiphany in which, suddenly "inspired by the absolute hopelessness of everything," he envisages a new world where he can burrow fully and freely into life. As usual, he writes of the experience in terms of a symbolism both powerful and stridently abstruse:

I made up my mind that I would hold on to nothing, that I would expect nothing, that henceforth I would live as an animal, a beast of prey, a rover, a plunderer. . . . At this very moment, in the quiet dawn of a new day was not the earth giddy with crime and distress? Had one single element of man's nature been altered, vitally, fundamentally altered, by the incessant march of history? . . . I have reached the limits of endurance. . . . The world which I have departed is a menagerie. The dawn is breaking on a new world, a jungle world in which the lean spirits roam with sharp claws. If I am a hyena I am a lean and hungry one: I go forth to fatten myself. (100–101)

All this quasi-mystical self-aggrandizing is as much pompous posturing for an effect as it is a serious attempt to find proper expression for an ever-recurring sense of hopelessness. But then, considering Miller's point of departure, what else could we expect? The scene Miller had been describing occurs, not surprisingly, in a brothel where, perhaps despite his better judgment, he had conducted a rather dandified and panting disciple of Gandhi's. The young Hindu, despite his eagerness, is obviously out of his depth. Turning his head away and blushing violently, he asks Miller to do the choosing from among the "bevy of naked women" surrounding them. Then, in an awkward violation of decorum, he has Miller switch girls with him. Finally, he commits the ultimate *faux pas* in confusing the functions of the *bidet* and the toilet—and it is the resultant unflushable mess which actuates Miller's readily stimulated imagination, for he freely associates it not merely with his erstwhile companion, but with all disciples of any faith, and hence with all of man's hopes for a better life either in this world or in the next. Miller believes not only that things are rotten, but that they are bound to get a good deal worse. And thus his incessant wallowing in filth and degradation, the so-called seamier aspects of life, as a kind of objective correlative for his despair.

One of the would-be burners of *Cancer* has said that it is " 'like a slut walking down a neighborhood street, half undressed and spewing filth to those near her,' and that it 'deals heavily with carnal experiences, with perversion, with human filth and excrement'."[24] Deal with these things it does, of course, yet such a statement is misleading. For one thing, sexual perversion occurs rarely in Miller's fiction (unlike, for instance, Lawrence Durrell in his never-banned *Alexandria Quartet*, Miller is not fascinated by in-

---

[24] Jack Mabley, quoted in " 'Cancer' in Chicago," p. 9.

cest and homosexuality). At one point in *Cancer* he even expresses
revulsion at a friend's espousal of masturbation, and in *Capricorn*,
describing a boyhood attack on a sissy of a choirboy, he says, "it was
a disgraceful performance, but it made us feel good. Nobody knew
yet what a fairy was, but whatever it was we were against it" (135).

Even his seemingly endless pursuit of females—or, more precisely, of the sex organs of prostitutes—must be examined in context; for, although obviously obsessed with the *idea* of sex, Miller,
especially in *Cancer*, is largely indifferent to it in reality. Despite
his concern with his physical needs, he almost never goes out of
his way to satisfy them. Taking a woman to bed—although he does
so at every opportunity—seems always to be someone else's idea:
the various women who accost him in the streets or the cafes, the
blushing Hindu afraid to go upstairs alone, the friend who offers
him the loan of his own latest bed-mate. Miller's reaction to the
latter is typical: "I didn't know whether I wanted to or not," he
says, but of course he does (279). It is free, it is convenient, and
besides it saves him the cost of a night's lodging.

Miller's essential passivity regarding sex receives full treatment
much earlier in *Cancer*. He is with Van Norden, an agreeably un-
savory character who functions as a kind of alter ego, and who, in
contrast with Miller, literally does think and talk of nothing but
sex. Bessie, the only woman he cannot take to bed, correctly characterizes him as "just a worn-out satyr" who does not "know the
meaning of passion" (p. 135). With Miller in tow, he engages for
both of them the invariable nameless and hungry prostitute. The
three of them, all equally passionless, retire to Van Norden's room,
where Miller's passivity casts him into the role of *voyeur*. "As I
watch Van Norden tackle her," he writes,

it seems to me that I'm looking at a machine whose cogs have slipped.
. . . I am sitting on a chair behind him, watching their movements with
a cool, scientific detachment. . . . It's like watching one of those crazy
machines which throw the newspaper out. . . . The machine seems more
sensible, crazy as it is, and more fascinating to watch, than the human

beings and the events which produced it. My interest in Van Norden and the girl is nil. . . . As long as that spark of passion is missing there is no human significance in the performance. The machine is better to watch (143).

Here, undoubtedly, is the crux of Miller's problem, for his sexual passivity and general malaise result from that absent spark of passion. In general, as we have seen, he attempts to make the sterility of the world about him into the villain of the piece—even to the point of faulting Paris, the one place where life has been possible for him. At times, however, Miller will attempt a more specific self-analysis, a more intimate delving after the roots of the cancerous growths within him. Of a much earlier period he writes: "things were wrong usually only when one cared too much. That impressed itself on me very early in life. . . . This caring too much— I remember that it only developed with me about the time I first fell in love. And even then I didn't care enough. If I had really cared I wouldn't be here now writing about it. . . . It was a bad experience because it taught me how to live a lie" (*Capricorn*, 14–15).

The Miller of the *Tropics*, then, is a man who has trained himself to care for no one—and rather than run the risks of emotional involvement attendant upon normal human intercourse, he reduces all such contact to the simply sexual. Concomitantly, when every woman becomes a whore and every whore a single anatomical feature, the process, as Miller has suggested, is a lie, or rather, the poetic technique of synecdoche. Like food, then, the simple animalistic response to sexual stimulus serves as a safe standard, for it actually involves only a minute fraction of the real personality buried beneath the brutish exterior.

But the buffoon-lecher mask slips occasionally, revealing a Miller who cares very much indeed. For throughout the autobiographical fiction, as Kingsley Widmer has indicated, there runs the pivotal theme of

the misery and inspiration connected with the Dark Lady of passion.

She is partly the *femme fatale* of the romantic, an inverted traditional muse of the artist, the Eve-Lilith of primordial knowledge, a witch-goddess of sexuality and power, and, according to Miller's insistence, his second wife. Under the names of Mona and Mara, she haunts most of Miller's work; and she appears, at least briefly, in almost every book he has written.[25]

Certainly her appearances are brief and intermittent, for her story is as fragmented as everything else in Miller's discontinuous narrative. Nonetheless, Miller's treatment of her constantly emphasizes her emotional centrality to his life and to his work. For one thing, the Mona/Mara passages are remarkably free of both censorable language and excremental references. Descriptions of Mona and of scenes with her, unlike those of the other women in the *Tropics*, never become flights of nihilistic, semiabstract imagery indulged in for their own sake. Of the significance of Mona, the "Her" to whom *Capricorn* is dedicated, Miller writes: "Everything I endured was in the nature of a preparation for that moment when, putting on my hat one evening, I walked out of the office, out of my hitherto private life, and sought the woman who was to liberate me from a living death" (64).

In *Cancer* she appears initially as a figure of almost virginal purity, a kind of antiwhore who embodies love rather than sex. Miller has been eagerly awaiting her return to Paris when "suddenly," he writes,

I see a pale heavy face with burning eyes—and the little velvet suit that I always adored because under the soft velvet there were always her warm breasts, the marble legs, cool, firm, muscular. She rises up out of a sea of faces and embraces me, embraces me passionately. . . . I sit down beside her and she talks—a flood of talk. . . . I hear not a word because she is beautiful and I love her and now I am happy and willing to die (27).

[25] Widmer, *Henry Miller*, p. 69.

Then in bed their intense passion finds expression, as do Miller's tenderness and love—and a new emotion, fear.

She lies down on the bed with her clothes on. Once, twice, three times, four times . . . I'm afraid she'll go mad . . . in bed, under the blankets, how good to feel her body again! But for how long? Will it last this time? Already I have a presentiment that it won't. . . . Finally she drops off and I pull my arm from under her. My eyes close. Her body is there beside me . . . it will be there till morning surely. . . . My eyes are closed. We breathe warmly into each other's mouth. Close together, America three thousand miles away. I never want to see it again. To have her here in bed with me, breathing on me, her hair in my mouth—I count that something of a miracle. Nothing can happen now till morning." (28)

But in the morning everything happens. They wake to find each other crawling with bedbugs; Mona, needing a bath, food, and adequate clothing, loses her temper at Miller's having forgotten to provide for money; and, although Miller does not detail the rest of the sequence of events, by the next page Mona disappears from the narrative—not to be even mentioned again for some 120 pages. Again he longs for her, wondering how different life might be with "a young, restless creature by [his] side"; but his image of her has altered drastically and, bitterly, he sees her as alien to his European world. If she ever should return, he wryly speculates,

she'll probably tell me right away that it's unsanitary. That's the first thing that strikes an American woman about Europe—that it's unsanitary. Impossible for them to conceive of a Paradise without modern plumbing. . . . She'll say I've become a degenerate. I know her line from beginning to end. She'll want to look for a studio with a garden attached —and a bath-tub to be sure. She wants to be poor in a romantic way. I know her. But I'm prepared for her this time. (151)

Exactly what is good about being poor in an unromantic way Miller never explains, but certainly he is correct about being pre-

pared for her—for he manages, at least for the moment, to blot
from his mind everything that belongs to the past, especially those
few years when they were together and life was, if not edenic, at
least vital and intense. Now when he thinks of her—and he is unable to keep himself from doing so entirely—it is "not as of a person in a definite aura of time and space, but separate, detached, as
though she had blown up into a great cloud-like form that blotted
out the past." Regardless, he adds,

I couldn't allow myself to think about her very long; if I had I would
have jumped off the bridge. It's strange. I had become so reconciled to
this life without her; and yet if I thought about her only for a minute
it was enough to pierce the bone and marrow of my contentment and
shove me back again into the agonizing gutter of my wretched past.
(175)

And yet, no matter what the reason, a man who wilfully destroys
his past, as Miller begins to realize, commits spiritual suicide: "It
seems as if my own proper existence had come to an end somewhere, just where exactly I can't make out. I'm not an American
any more, nor a New Yorker, and even less a European, or a Parisian. I haven't any allegiance, any responsibilities, any hatreds,
any worries, any prejudices, any passion. I'm neither for nor
against. I'm a neutral" (*Cancer*, p. 151). But this statement serves
first as manifesto and only subsequently as actual fact, for after the
climactic moment when he recognizes the irrevocable loss of Mona,
he gives way to a despairing loneliness so profound and so terrible
that all else seems irrelevant. Yet in his hopelessness he comes full
cycle, rediscovering his affinity with all the sordid and cancerous
aspects of Paris, a city that "attracts the tortured, the hallucinated,
the great maniacs of love," A Paris that "is like a whore. From a distance she seems ravishing, you can't wait until you have her in
your arms. And five minutes later you feel empty, disgusted with
yourself. You feel tricked" (178, 204). Ultimately, there are only
the streets for refuge, for the streets take every man's torments,

every man's raging despair that is so precious because it confirms his significance as an individual capable of suffering, and the streets make of it something neither for nor against, but simply neutral. Miller, as we see him last, is a vastly diminished figure wondering "in a vague way what had ever happened to [his] wife" (305). "A vague way"—the phrase is significant—for it suggests, and this is borne out in the later writings, that the failure of the relationship may well have resulted from Miller's intrinsic inadequacies. As Widmer has put it: "While his version of the Dark Lady myth aims to show Miller as the victim of love, he really presents himself as the victim of his own lovelessness."[26]

Thus Miller's passionless passivity, his apathetic indifference to the things that most of us value in life. He begins his *Tropics* triad as a rebel without a cause—as "a James Dean character, a Hemingway of undisciplined creative yearnings"[27]—and even though he is often ludicrous and ineffectual we are sympathetic, for he is saying things that need to be said; we have heard them before, but they bear the repeating. For, as Miller puts it in *Capricorn*, "even if everything I say is wrong, is prejudiced, spiteful, malevolent, even if I am a liar and a poisoner, it is nonetheless the truth and it will have to be swallowed" (13).

Before very long, however, he is worn out and used up, a causeless nonconformist maintaining the old postures merely because they have become habitual. By the end of *Cancer*, Miller has even run out of defiant gestures. He is sitting in a cafe, idly watching the Seine; his pockets are bulging with money—the filthy stuff he has always claimed to despise—money, moreover, he has stolen from a friend. And, perhaps strangest and unkindest cut of all, he speaks the tired conservatism of the *nouveau riche*: ". . . you can't create a revolution," he writes. "You can't wash *all* the dirt out of your belly" (*Cancer*, p. 304). Thus in *Capricorn* Miller has nowhere to go. "To want to change the condition of affairs," he writes at the

26 *Ibid.*, p. 75.
27 Gertz, *Critics*, p. 177.

beginning of that book, "seemed futile to me; nothing would be altered, I was convinced, except by a change of heart, and who could change the hearts of men?" (9). Miller had thought that he could, but he was wrong. "For a man of my temperament," he adds later in the same book, "the world being what it is, there is absolutely no hope, no solution" (102).

Miller claims that the *Tropics* are about regeneration—"the Dionysian theme which . . . must be the theme for the writers to come —the only theme permissible, or possible."[28] Miller does occasionally employ redemptive imagery—for example, the quietly flowing Seine at the end of *Cancer*—but he seems ultimately incapable of rising from negation to affirmation, incapable of transcending his long dark night of the soul (the very word "soul," in fact, he finds ludicrous). In *Capricorn* he writes that "whoever, through too great love, which is monstrous after all, dies of his misery, is born again to know neither love nor hate, but to enjoy. And this joy of living, because it is unnaturally acquired, is a poison which eventually vitiates the whole world" (67–68). The *Tropics*, then, is not about redemption at all, but only about the death of love—and the irrevocable finality and waste of one man's spiritual suicide.

Certainly only the naïve would attempt to deny that love has indeed pitched its mansion in the place of excrement, but only those uncompromisingly bitter and self-defeating—and Miller is both in these books—attempt to exalt an excremental or merely animalistic standard over that of love. Miller, it seems, would have the cancerous growths of his *Tropics* block out the light entering love's mansion, just as his own memory conveniently blotted out more and more of his painful past. But fortunately, and perhaps despite his intentions, Miller demonstrates that such a perverse disordering is invariably doomed to failure—and this demonstration may well be the one permanent edifice in the jungles of Henry Miller's *Tropics*.

[28] Henry Miller, in Durrell and Miller, *Correspondence*, p. 78. Miller is speaking specifically of Lawrence Durrell's *The Black Book*, but, by implication, about his own books as well.

Androgynes Bound:
Nathanael West's **Miss Lonelyhearts**

Roger D. Abrahams

Nathanael West's short novel *Miss Lonelyhearts*, in spite of its brevity, is one of the most demanding and perplexing reading experiences of American letters. This work utilizes a totally ironic perspective while telling a story of a very real moral dilemma in psychologically realistic terms, thereby forcing the reader to sympathize with the title character and to laugh at him at the same time. It is a work of utter despair, yet its ironic approach causes despair itself to be branded ridiculous. Throughout, we are asked to identify with one who cannot himself find identification and whose name we never know.

Our perplexity is compounded by the novel's history. Written in the depression years, yet in a style more characteristic of the twenties, the life view presented seems closer to the era after World War II. Perhaps this is why it is only since the issuance of his collected novels in 1957 that West has received widespread critical and popular attention.

Miss Lonelyhearts is a work primarily concerned with the individual's moral and psychological struggle in a world in which all values are suspect, and all attempts to achieve identity are subject to frustration. It examines many systems of thought and action and rejects them all as illusory. Possibilities of help, perfection, and hope are dangled before our eyes and then dashed on the rocks of disillusion. Even with such successive defeats, the importance of the continuance of the search is never questioned.

In this regard the book seems to be built much like Nathanael West himself—at least the West described by his friend Malcolm Cowley:

To avoid the danger of being solemn he used to stick pins in his dearest illusions. Nevertheless he kept having more of them, like a boy inflating

toy balloons from an inexhaustible store. . . . He was always called
"Pep," I don't know for what reason, but somehow the nickname was
fitting; it seemed to reveal a quality of continually wounded and revived innocence, as if he were everybody's kid brother.[1]

This pattern of "wounded and revived innocence" suffuses the life
of the title character, Miss Lonelyhearts. The wounding and the
reviving of innocence are equally important, for without the hope
of the innocent the wound will not be fully felt. The presence of
adversity, of chaos, is admitted then forgotten; an ideal of harmony
must be preserved in spite of adversity and even with the probability that it will never be realized in more than a personal and momentary way. Life cannot be fully experienced by retreat. This
persistence of the search in the midst of painful forbearance is a
pattern which is communicated in all of West's works. It is for good
reason that *Miss Lonelyhearts* appears to be a shaggy-dog story, an
elaborate tale about activity which seems to drive toward something,
only to be exposed as pointless, frustrated action.

One traditional shaggy-dog story reflects just such a frustration
pattern in content as well as form. Two rabbis have searched all
their lives for the secret of life. Having read all of the many wise
books on the subject and having found no answer, they finally turn
to meditation. One day one bursts into the other's sanctuary crying,
"I've found it." "You've found what?" "I've found the secret of
life." "You what? Tell me quickly; what have you found?" "Life,"
he said. "Life is like a butterfly." "Life is like a butterfly?" "So life
isn't like a butterfly."

In *Miss Lonelyhearts* the search is both internal and external.
The quest is made by one who perceives chaos both within himself
and in the outside world and who experiences the two inseparably in
his attempt to find order. In looking he is presented with a number
of traditional plans of action—some of society's "dearest illusions."

---

[1] Introduction to Avon Edition, *Miss Lonelyhearts* (New York: Avon Publica-
tions, 1959), ii–iii. This is the edition which I will use throughout, and page
references to it will be given in parentheses after a quotation.

Retreat to nature, mysticism, self-sacrifice, sentimental love, worldliness, and the life of total reason—all are explored, discussed, subjected to the cruelest kind of scrutiny, and then rejected. They are discarded not only because they are vanities and hypocrisies, but also because they do not fulfill the needs of Miss L to find either an answer to the inequities of the world or a slave for his wounded psyche.

I

Before scrutiny of the details of Miss Lonelyhearts' search, consideration of the nature of the novel is important. Even though such a widely read critic as Stanley Edgar Hyman states that this novel sprang into the world "with hardly a predecessor," the work derives its tone and patterns of expectations from some very important literary traditions. Simply from the point of view of stylistic effects, West owes a great deal to the symbolists and the surrealists.[2] His uniformly bleak, defoliated world shares a great deal with Eliot and many others writing in the twenties. More important, however, the structure of the work develops upon the techniques and expectation patterns of previous types of prose fiction.

Miss Lonelyhearts is a work which centers upon a central character floundering in the midst of an adverse moral climate and wrestling with problems of both psychological and ethical dimension. In delineating this situation the book draws upon at least three traditions for its vocabulary and point of view: satire, allegory, and the novel of psychological development. As in so many satires, a moral point of view is developed through the presentation of an innocent in the midst of the corrupt, corruption appearing that much more profound because it is presented by the naïve observer. Further, the innocent is shown to be fully as deluded and vain as the corrupt;

[2] For West's debt to the surrealists see James F. Light, *Nathanael West: An Interpretive Study* (Evanston, Illinois: Northwestern University Press, 1961), pp. 37–39, 93–97. I am indebted to this interpretive biography for much information and many insights.

just as we discover that such satiric protagonists as Gulliver and Candide are the dupes of their own insular systems of thought, so Miss Lonelyhearts is revealed to be deluded by his mystical sentimentalism.

In regard to the moral dimension *Miss Lonelyhearts* utilizes some of the techniques of allegory as well as those of satire. The novel presents us with a central Everyman type character and a number of "flat," subsidiary characters who vie for his soul. Each of the arguers represents a single point of view, a force which is also part of the inner struggle of the protagonist.

Satire and allegory provide techniques drawn upon by many novels of psychological development, and it is this subgenre which is of greatest importance in the construction of *Miss Lonelyhearts*. This type of fiction centers upon a gifted but incomplete individual and his struggle to become whole. Derived from the confessional tradition, and strongly influenced by Dostoievski, works in this pattern have provided some of the high spots of the twentieth-century novel. Such writers as Joyce, Kafka, Thomas Wolfe, and Beckett, to mention only a few, have been known primarily for this kind of fiction. In all, interest is focused upon the unformed or malformed mind's progress in attempting to attain balance, satisfaction, and insight into self and the external world. Interest resides in psychic struggle. We are generally presented with an individual who, because of the largeness of spirit and an ability to perceive farther and deeper than others, recognizes his isolation. This engenders internal conflicts, for in order to act on these perceptions the individual must achieve some kind of *rapprochement* with the outside world, must make some kind of compromise and must develop a vocabulary, so that communication becomes possible. He is often shown to have capacities of feeling and perception but an inability to organize and effectively express or act on his insights. Until he can do so, he will not achieve his true identity. The experiences which the protagonist undergoes, and their effect on him, determine whether identity will be achieved.

There are two possible attacks on this problem of identity in this sort of novel. In the "artist as young man" type, the pattern is similar to that of a romance: the hero becomes temporarily isolated from society on an active quest of self and the sources of his being. Such works, generally written in the spirit of retrospection, depict experience as causal and progressive and purposive, leading to the present artist-figure. Internal tensions, which are only temporary, are eliminated in moments of vision in which the hero suddenly perceives a unity of the internal and external worlds. The tone of such fictions is usually optimistic.

Miss Lonelyhearts is obviously not of this type. It is more firmly one of the second variety of novels of psychological development, one we might call the "existential," the "chaotic experience," or the anti-romance novel. Here isolation is a permanent condition; the progress of the psyche, if there is any, is toward more intensive isolation, perhaps death. The tone of such works is ironic. Moments occur which might have become revelatory but which fail to transform the protagonist or resolve his problems. Consequently, the protagonist is never able to achieve the object of his search, the ability to act. He is immobilized. The search becomes a wait. This kind of progression characterizes *Miss Lonelyhearts*. The fixed moral and psychological dilemma of man is morbidly attractive; his search for answers is necessary but futile. We are given the situation and expectation pattern of the "artist as young man" type, but they are used ironically.

II

After the publication of *Miss Lonelyhearts* West wrote a piece on his novelistic technique. In it he said, "The novelist is no longer a psychologist. Psychology can become much more important. The great body of case histories can be used in the way the ancient writers used their myths. Freud is your Bullfinch; you can learn from him."[3] Psychologists have articulated for the novelist the archetypal dramas of human existence; the novelist may then use these "stories" as he wishes, freed of the necessity to observe the minutiae of the psychic life. West uses Freud in this way in *Miss Lonelyhearts*. The focal character is portrayed as a neurotic through whose psychic conflict the dimensions of man's condition can be measured. The details of his neurosis are given occasionally, but only to create a feeling of internal verisimilitude or to introduce a metaphor of structural importance. This is not a novel of psychological realism.

The central figure, Miss Lonelyhearts, finds himself in a neurotic state because he cannot effect a compromise between a life of reason and a life of feeling. He sees suffering all about him, and he sees this as evidence of chaos. Under the cloud of irreconcilable conflict and intuitions of chaos, he is driven into an escape world, the world of euphoric experience. Even there his tensions assert themselves, but in symbolic terms. But in his dreams or visions he finds solutions, resolutions, which he cannot find in the course of external life.

The psychoanalyst Wilhelm Stekel described this neurotic retreat in a metaphor which West himself uses throughout the book: "The polyphony of thought draws its energy out of the organs. In the [neurotic], the psychic and physical equilibrium is disturbed. Disharmonies make life unbearable for him. He belongs more to dreams than reality. He hearkens to the middle voices."[4] This is certainly an accurate description of the pattern of Miss Lonelyhearts' experience. Whenever he encounters a difficult interpersonal problem which demands a solution dictated by him, he retreats to the noisy isolation of the speakeasy or to the impregnable fortress of his bed. Eventually, even his bed-hideaway is discovered, and he finds that he must erect a wall around himself so that the outside world cannot assault him with its spoon-fed soup and its easy ad-

---

[3] Quoted in Light, *An Interpretive Study*, p. 96, from West's article, "Some Notes on *Miss Lonelyhearts*," *Contempo* (May 15, 1933), p. 2.

[4] Wilhelm Stekel, *Sadism and Masochism*, trans. Louise Brink, Volume I, Evergreen Edition (New York: Grove Press, 1963), p. 21.

vice. He becomes a "rock" impervious to the incursion of the "sea."
("What goes on in the sea is of no interest to the rock" [87].)

But Miss L's neurotic state is the center of a universe which is
immobilized by this internal conflict. As one of the faceless drinkers
in the speakeasy observes, while commenting on Miss L's dilemma,
"The trouble with him, the trouble with all of us, is that we have
no outer life, only an inner one, and that by necessity" (27). Miss
L's sickness, the progress of the retreat from life because of anxiety,
provides West with the superstructure of his novel; texturing materials are the metaphors and images which arise from the music of
the "middle voices," the euphoric escape experiences of his antihero.

The pathos of Miss Lonelyhearts' condition is that he knows that
he is sick, but he finds that he can do nothing about it. He does not
always retreat from the situation. Though he cannot actively find
an answer to his problem, he does allow himself to be preached at,
spoon-fed, led by the hand to the speakeasy, the country, the bed;
he seems to hope that someone will show him the way. The dominant dramatic pattern of the work is an alternation between encounters with life in which someone else tries to show him a program for the solution of his problems and a retreat into himself in
which the problem is worked out in his unconscious.

Miss L recognizes that the basis of his malaise is his inability to
fuse feeling and sense into an attitude or an effective program of
action. In internal terms he cannot harmonize the dictates of head
with those of heart. He cannot abstract himself from his feelings
and thus go about acting on them. He is pulled apart by these po-
larities and has only intuitions of order in the midst of chaos. This
order-chaos problem exists in the external world as well, for the
adversity with which he is in constant contact exists as an element
of the forces of destruction and dissolution. Naturally, not being
able to solve his internal problems, he cannot begin to give advice
to others on solving their external ones. Thus adversity, pictured
so dramatically in the letters he receives, only activates his own in-

ternal disorder. The correspondence helps him to externalize his problem, but then his inability to assist only further frustrates him. Failing to help in any way, he becomes incapable of action on any level of his life. Chaos reigns.

In characteristically neurotic fashion, he fights chaos by developing an "insane sensitiveness to order" (20). He looks to those who appear to have ordered lives, and he offers to let one or another lead him. Each time, he finally recognizes that all order is only transitory. In the depth of one of his "fevers" he sees clearly that chaos is part of the very essence of the external world and that order must come from within to be even momentarily effective. He phantasizes that he is in the midst of a pawnshop window, viewing "the paraphernalia of suffering," the furniture of chaos. He comes to realize that

man has a tropism for order. Keys in one pocket, change in another. Mandolins are tuned GDAE. The physical world has a tropism for disorder, entropy. Man against nature . . . the battle of the centuries. Keys yearn to mix with change. Mandolins strive to get out of tune. Every order has within it the germs of destruction. (51)

Thus he projects his problem in terms of a cosmic dialectic, recognizing that to be human and sane he must find a rational organizing principle.

But the order he searches for is not one of things, but of experience which will enable him to guide future action. He needs a program of action which will synthesize the dictates of heart and head. The conventionally accepted systems of order he is offered he finds unacceptable, incomplete, and inconsistent with these inner needs. But he can't find an answer within himself either.

The result is an inability to act, think, even write the letters demanded by his job. He is immobilized and muted. When he tries to talk, he finds that "his tongue . . . [has] become a fat thumb" (21). His only release from the tensions created by the need to communicate and the inability to do so is in sadistic action, retreat into self, or a passive resignation to the wishes of others.

Consequently, when he does act, it is not in line with any program but simply in blind *re*action. Actions become only twitch-rejections, nothing more. He wants to have a purpose, to advance into life, but because of his lack of confidence and self-control he retreats from others, becoming submerged periodically in the fevered world of his own making. He engages with another only when the other takes the initiative. "Like a dead man, only friction could make him warm or violence make him mobile" (34). He occasionally has life rubbed into him, but each time his inner conflicts force him to turn on those who have forced him out of his cell. This rejection adds to the depth of the defeat, deepening his sense of chaos, loss of control, and isolation.

This pattern of rejection is felt very strongly by Miss L because it represents a failure of heart. His heart dictates acceptance, not rejection. It is only in his fantasy world that this acceptance principle ever seems to be effected, and at those few moments internal harmony is achieved.

III

Miss Lonelyhearts' rejection of the life-programs which are offered to him by others occurs because each lacks this ability to harmonize through acceptance. The two attitudes most persistently injected into Miss L's life are those of cynicism and optimistic sentimentalism. The cynic interprets the world as corrupt and would ignore or cast doubt on all evidence to the contrary. To protect himself against the incursions of this corruption he erects a barrier of reasoned noninvolvement in which control of life is achieved through the recognition of its dominant pattern and the development of psychic detachment. The sentimentalist on the other hand sees life as purposive and good. He would ignore evil or inequity and construct a world in which only goodness and beauty and happiness would find place. Both, then, would arbitrarily limit experience, one in favor of the head; the other, the heart.

In allegorical fashion one character represents monistically each of these points of view.[5] Shrike is the complete cynic; Betty, the total pastoral sentimentalist. Both argue as prophets of "the true way" in an attempt to convince Miss L. But Miss L recognizes the restrictive quality of both points of view in their tendency to forget important areas of life. Miss L says this of Betty: "Her world was not the world and could never include the readers of his column. Her sureness was based on the power to limit experience arbitrarily" (21). The same could be said of Shrike, but Miss L never takes him seriously enough to comment on his cynical approach. Though Miss L is confused, and they do not seem to be, his "confusion was significant, while [their] order was not" (21). Both Shrike and Betty would ignore suffering, accepting arbitrary order as truth. The order for which Miss L searches must come from inclusiveness and total acceptance, not exclusiveness and rejection. It must be a unity of disparate parts.

Shrike and Betty are the two most important people in the life of Miss L. They are the ones who most frequently rub him into life. Both see that he is wracked by confusion and indecision and see this as a sign of innocence, naïveté, and immaturity. Each talks to him as if he were a child, Shrike speaking as if he were his father, Betty, his mother. Both want him to become a man, though they differ radically on what such a step would mean. Ultimately, Miss L's rejection of them and their points of view occurs because he recognizes that theirs are worlds of their own creation, childish fantasy worlds. They, not he, are the ones in need of growing up.

Furthermore, each is not what he seems to be. Shrike likes to por-

---

[5] Throughout the following discussion of characters I am indebted in certain particulars to Light, *An Interpretive Study*, pp. 79–83, and Stanley Edgar Hyman, *Nathanael West* (No. 21, University of Minnesota Pamphlets on American Writers, Minneapolis, 1962), pp. 17–19. I differ from both writers in most regards, however, Light being a bit simplistic and Hyman often wrongheaded.

tray himself in paternal terms, as a phallically superior male, one with control and authority. His control is too reliant on his rapier-sharp handling of words; in actions he is a failure. Ultimately he is unmasked as feckless and impotent—his phallicism only degenerate sadism. With his own wife, sex is impossible; with the ever available, faceless Rose Farkis, his caresses are dispassionate and calculated, his kiss, the burying of his "triangular face like the blade of a hatchet in her neck" (15).

Betty imagines herself a country maiden, an earth-mother, a symbol of fecundity. However, it soon becomes evident that she has anesthetized herself to the sensual side of life. Not even Miss L's sadistic pluck at her roselike nipple can stir her. The profundities of birth or death mean nothing to her. Though seduced and pregnant at the end of the story, she continues to think and act like a virgin. Her fecund sexuality resolves itself into little more than a casual masochism. She is not like any animal of the fields, easily available in the matter of increase; rather, she is "like a kitten whose soft helplessness makes one ache to hurt it" (23).

Betty and Shrike are paired against each other vying for Miss L's allegiance throughout this work, and their images are projected in contrasting terms. Not only are the male-female, paternal-maternal, sadism-masochism dichotomies employed in defining their roles, but also the split between city and country. Shrike is the man of the city with all the attendant traits of world-weariness and sophistication, while Betty is the innocent country girl without wile.

The city reflects the most vicious and sadistic, the most defeated aspects of life. The most recurrent symbol of this attitude is the little park which Miss L sits in or walks through so often. It is first described in the most agonizing terms:

He entered the park at the North Gate and swallowed mouthfuls of the heavy shade that curtained its arch. He walked into the shadow of a lamp-post that lay on the path like a spear. It pierced him like a spear.

As far as he could discover, there were no signs of spring. The decay that covered the surface of the mottled ground was not the kind in which

life generates. Last year, he remembered, May had failed to quicken
these soiled fields. It had taken all the brutality of July to torture a few
green spikes through the exhausted dirt. (10)

This wasteland is as theatrically and sadistically castratory as
Shrike. In one description the same defeated sexuality becomes even
more pronounced, for the park comes to life and is exhibitionist-
ically autoerotic.

. . . when he reached the little park he slumped down on a bench opposite the Mexican War obelisk.
   The stone shaft cast a long, rigid shadow on the walk in front of him.
He sat staring at it without knowing why until he noticed that it was
lengthening in rapid jerks, not as shadows usually lengthen. He grew
frightened and looked up quickly at the monument. It seemed red and
swollen in the dying sun, as though it were about to spout a load of
granite seed. (33)

   Betty argues true country values and finally persuades Miss L to
visit a farm owned by her aunt. In the country the sodden fruitless
valley of the city springs into perspective, and he is partially revived and duped by the country air, the owls, the loons, and the
deer. He is even able to eat an apple with Betty and take a fall with
her on the earth, ignoring his perception that the life-process was
little better off in the country than in the city: ". . . they went for
a walk in the woods. It was very sad under the trees. Although
spring was well advanced, in the deep shade there was nothing but
death—rotten leaves, gray and white fungi, and over everything a
funereal hush" (62). Both worlds are tainted with the smells of
decay and death at the very times when life should be asserting itself. But the country world seems to be calmly accepting this condition, while the city is actively proselytizing for it. Miss L really
only wants "to cultivate his interior garden" (27) anyway. The
two worlds reflect the values of their defenders. Betty sees the corruption of the city; Shrike, the "dull" quality (55) of the country,
but neither can see the sterility of their own worlds.

Betty, for all her country ideals, is really nothing but the great American housewife. Her order is based on social decorum, the straightening of the tie or the wearing of the gingham apron, not on the primal course of the cycle of nature. She can't stand smells, especially human ones, and that is her real reason for rejecting the city. The suburbs would really fill the bill.

In her own way Betty is an avatar of the girl nextdoor, the sentimental one who feels a fateful quality in her loving, but who never really loves. Her sentimental approach has her submerged in feeling, but experiencing no passion, "all heart and no genitals."[6] To be sure, she "gives herself" to Miss L, but not through any primal attraction. Rather, she wants to save him, redeem him, and order his life by putting his slippers by the crackling fire so that he'll be comfortable when he comes home at night. She firmly accepts the American belief that women are the center of the moral universe, placed on earth to bring order to men. Any man is redeemable so long as the right woman comes along. Miss L rejects her and her world twice, not with guilt, but with annoyance "at having been fooled into thinking that such a solution was possible" (22). In his final mood of acceptance he does say that he will marry her since she is pregnant, but by then he has become the impervious rock in such a state of mind that nothing can disturb him.

If Betty is "all heart and no genitals," Shrike is all head and false genitals. He is the vilifier of Greek comedy, carrying with him his bludgeon; or he is the court fool, exuding wit and badinage, carrying his false staff by which he parodies the king. But strangely, he takes himself seriously, acting as though his authority were real, speaking as if he represented truth. Fortunately, Miss L accepts Shrike's verbiage as trivial, his authority as assailable. Shrike never becomes more than a lord of misrule, an agent of chaos in a world turned upside down.

[6] Leslie Fiedler, *Love and Death in the American Novel* (New York: Criterion Books, 1960). Fiedler's analysis of this character type in American fiction I have found to be particularly provocative.

One of Shrike's favorite roles is that of anti-Christ devil. His name, beyond referring to the sadistic bird who impales his prey on thorns, is almost an anagram on the name of Christ. He is the man who sees himself as the bearer of the word, but his cynicism and basically destructive nature reveal him to be the false Messiah. His position an anti-Christ is made evident in the first lines of the book where he parodies the litany "Anima Christi" in the manner of the Black Mass, a calumny that reoccurs in other forms throughout the book.

> Soul of Miss L, glorify me.
> Body of Miss L, nourish me.
> Blood of Miss L, intoxicate me.
> Tears of Miss L, wash me. . . . (1)

He articulates the "Gospel according to Shrike" (89) and posits a new style trinity composed of "Father, Son and Wirehaired Fox Terrier" (58).

Shrike's badinage is mere show; when confronted in his home, he admits to inabilities with his wife, blaming her, of course. He claims that "sleeping with her is like sleeping with a knife in one's groin." This is probably true. From what we know of Mary, she is the perfect mate for Shrike. She, too, is dispassionate, frigid, a tease who talks freely but who is incapable of action. Everything about her is sadistically calculated to attract and frustrate men. If Shrike is a parody Messiah, she is a travesty of the Virgin, eternal symbol of miraculous fecundity. She allows Miss L to rub against her, even to undress her in the hall, but never to have coitus with her. Her manner of dress is a perfect reflection of her painful seductiveness: "She was wearing a tight, shiny dress that was like glass-covered steel and there was something cleanly mechanical in her pantomime" (39). She is as dehumanized and insensate as her husband.

Though Mary and Betty are opposed in most respects, they share sexual anesthesia. Each leaves Miss L feeling unfulfilled and empty because of their easy limitation of experience. Fay Doyle represents a further incomplete mode of life. She has neither head nor heart, only a body and a physical drive which she inflicts on the docile Miss L. She is totally primal, and her drive is given is cosmic terms. Her breath is "sea sounds," her call, a "sea-moan," her rhythm of life, "moon-driven" (47). Even her way of speaking is hypnotic and incantatory in its "tom-tom" rhythm. Her speech shows a failure of both heart and head in its lack of common sense or logic and its revelation of casual bigotry. After her initial seduction of Miss L, in which he willingly reverses roles with her, she, too, is rejected because of her limited approach to life.

Her husband, Peter Doyle, mirrors the deepest of Miss L's problems. He, too, is a real lonelyheart, crippled by life, needing love so badly that he is willing to go to ridiculous extremes to get it. Whereas Miss L is an emotional cripple, Peter is physically deformed. Fay Doyle causes both of them to assume the passive role, Peter going even farther than Miss L, once becoming a lap dog. Both are muted by their infirmities, Peter perhaps more completely so.

When the cripple finally labored into speech, Miss Lonelyhearts was unable to understand him. He listened hard for a few minutes and realized that Doyle was making no attempt to be understood. He was giving birth to groups of words that lived inside of him as things, a jumble of retorts he had meant to make when insulted and the private curses against fate that experience had taught him to swallow. (75)

Miss L recognizes the bond between himself and Peter and in so doing feels a sudden strength and compassion. In a real act of love he takes Peter by the hand while sitting in the speakeasy and tries to convey through his continued touch the depth of his understanding and love. Peter never understands, however, and eventually becomes the instrument of Miss L's death.

IV

It is the vision of the possibility of love as a unifying force which provides Miss L with his ability to persist throughout the work. He associates love with Christ and at certain important times tries to make himself over in Christ's image. He says to Betty, "I've got a Christ complex . . . Humanity . . . I'm a humanity lover." This means a number of things in this book. At times it seems to imply that he sees himself as the impaled Christ, the Man of Sorrows dying for the sins of the world. More often, however, it is Christ as unifier, Christ as Saviour, Prince of Love, that dominates, but this is when unity visits him in his vision, not when he goes out to capture control of life. In his own room he lives like a priest, and it is there that Christian deliverance occurs through meditation on the figure of the crucified Saviour. But when he tries to become a priest in the outside world, with his correspondents or with Peter and Fay Doyle, he becomes mute and ineffective. Love may work when it dictates to the individual, but as the basis for a program of interaction it is doomed, this parable seems to tell us.

But the principle of Love is the only one that Miss L can accept, because it is the only one which takes into account all of the contradictory forces of human experience and gives them order. Two interrelated problems which Miss L learns to cope with through love are violence and sexuality.

The vocabulary of violence dominates this novel.[7] From the letters to the newspaper at the beginning, to the final, meaningless shooting at the end, the work expresses its deepest intuitions of chaotic life in terms of destruction. Miss L feels this violence strongly, but he has learned to cope with it neither in the outside world nor in his own nature. He recognizes that violence as destruction is akin to chaos; while it exists, attempts at order are doomed.

Surely the reason why the letters describing adversity affect him so deeply is that he himself is capable of blindly destroying and thus causing adversity in the lives of others. But he is also capable of feeling deep guilt at the expression of this impulsive destruction, and he consequently places himself in a position where *he* will be

[7] Cf. Hyman, *Nathanael West*, pp. 19–20.

hurt. This alternation of attitudes is the sado-masochistic pattern, and it accounts for an important inner rhythm in the structure of this novel.

The work begins with the first of Shrike's savage onslaughts. This, combined with the effect of the unfathomable distress of his correspondents on his mood, seems to send Miss L into a state of savage depression. Following this are three scenes in which Miss L commences an act of love only to experience failure which causes the action to turn into sadistic violence. The first is a flashback. He is reminded of a youthful experience, of a time when he and some friends went to the woods to sacrifice a lamb. The ceremony soon deteriorated, for the knife they used broke, and they left the animal there bleeding to death. Later, Miss L returned and savagely kicked the rest of the life out of the lamb.

The next scene replays the sadistic destructive action on an innocent creature. Miss L goes to see Betty, whom he hasn't visited in two months, since they had first become engaged. His heart has failed him, and he calls up the instinct to hurt others in reprisal for his feeling of inner void. He treats her in a brutal fashion, assailing her both physically and mentally and leaves her in tears.

This scene is followed by another reminiscence—this time of two mass rapes of women, told in heartless terms. Then there is the most violent and sadistic scene of the work, once again illustrative of Miss L's basic pattern of the frustration of initial love impulse. After getting punched for being polite during a drinking spree in his speakeasy, Miss L and a friend go walking. In the wasteland park they spy a "clean, old man" in the comfort station. The man is the perfect outgrowth of this park, a harmless, feckless, castrato who mirrors many of Miss L's own failures and inabilities. They take pity on this man and invite him to have a drink, which he accepts. Then the two begin to give the man the third degree, and the performance becomes increasingly merciless. The grotesque man becomes mute with fright. Finally, Miss L insanely begins to twist the man's arm.

After this orgy of sadistic action, Miss L seems to undergo feelings of remorse. He immediately places himself in a position where he must be used, hurt, vilified. He invites Mary Shrike out, knowing that she will tease and then refuse him. Then he allows himself to be seduced by Fay Doyle. Thoroughly beaten, he retreats to his bed and to fevered visions of harmony in diversity. In such a state, Betty is able to persuade him to go to the farm, and the cycle begins once more, although not at such a violent level.

These sadistic and masochistic expressions are a reflection of Miss L's inner fears and emerge as demonstrations of hate. Hate is the drive to power and arises from a context of lack of control. Love is the ability to renounce hate and power and the will to submit to the demands of a higher organizing force (such as the family system, society, and God). This submission is totally different from that of masochism, for rather than being the expression of a will to control (in masochism, deflected from the external world back onto self destructively because of guilt), it is the renunciation of power. Not too strangely, Miss L finds that in the world of Shrike and Betty he cannot feel and act on love. They activate only those parts of his inner life which he fears, hates, and reacts against. Little wonder, then, that he retreats into himself and his cell of solitude when confronted by the demands of that life.

This problem with violence is closely related to Miss L's problems of sexual identity. Social norm dictates that a man is active in all realms of life, especially his relations with women. Similarly, men are supposed to act through the dictates of reason, by using their heads. This is the model of manliness which Shrike pretends to portray, and he very explicitly demands that Miss L emulate him in this respect. But by so demanding, Shrike creates a basic confusion in his relation with Miss L. He speaks from the vantage of authority and greater experience, treating Miss L as if he were a child. Thus, while demanding emulation, he is also insisting upon passive obedience. Shrike's role as authority figure and proposed ego-ideal, therefore, creates an initial conflict which is further complicated by the revelation that Shrike is not the superior male he pretends to be.

Betty, too, tries to reshape Miss L's world to conform to her values. She seems to argue that tidiness is of utmost importance, even if it involves retreat and docility in the face of adverse reality on both of their parts. If he will become the rightful provider, she will keep his bungalow world clean and orderly. But she, too, has an internal inconsistency in her approach, for though she preaches the senti-mental-masochistic approach to life, her assailable position only brings out the sadistic side of Miss L's nature, thus making him more of a man in Shrike's mold.

Both Betty's and Shrike's images of manliness are sexless, how-ever. Both demand a renunciation of the true coming together of the sexes in a love state for something much less. Only Fay allows him a truly sexual expression, but it is a totally infantile one—she makes of him a baby, forcing his head to her breast. This is closer to his ideal; he does find momentary pleasure in having her reverse the usual roles.

The sado-masochistic cycle is one of three parts: sadistic action, masochistic docility, and retreat to bed and isolation. This tripartite arrangement is also true of the available routes of sexual expression. One may become active and male, passive and female, or regressive and infantile. "The human being does not consist of man and wo-man, but of man, woman, and child."[8] Each of these components has attributes which are vital in the balance of human experience. Man is capable of abstract thought and of action on principle; wo-man, of feeling and intuitive sympathy; child, of living and acting in the context of beautiful innocence.

The shock of adverse experience provides Miss L and the others with their greatest problem and defines for them their approaches to life. The monism of each of the subsidiary characters is deter-mined in part by his handling of some shock provided by rejection

[8] Stekel, *Sadism and Masochism*, p. 143.

or some other adverse experience. Both Mary and Shrike are immobilized and desensitized by their confrontations with the fullness and duplicity of life. Mary punctuates her teasing rejection of Miss L by reminiscing about her mother's rejection of her through death from breast cancer—all this while allowing herself to be undressed. Shrike, somehow emasculated by experience in the past, allows this trauma to be constantly re-enacted by marrying frigid Mary. Fay, betrayed sexually, spends the rest of her life getting back at men by marrying Peter, a man she can hurt repeatedly. Peter, rejected by life in his disability, tries to acquire a protecting mother by marrying the already pregnant Fay, only to have her emphasize his impotence by her rude treatment of him and by her infidelities. Each chooses to re-enact traumatic experience in his own fixed pattern, some identifying with the mechanism of rejection and acting on it, the others, acquiescing, constantly replaying the initial experience of defeat.

Betty alone is not defeated by experience, and this is why she can assert more influence on Miss L. Her life pattern is determined by a rejection of experience and a permanent prolongation of the state of innocence. Her vision of perfection is, not surprisingly, the country world. In this she invokes a persistent American solution to the problem of the experience of life in society—retreat to the woods where one's self-sufficiency will assert itself under the ordering eye of Mother Nature. Her answer to the duality of head and heart is to regress to the childlike state of mind in which the potential of reasoned judgment has not yet arisen. Her resolution for the dichotomy of the sexes is to retreat to that period when such differences had not yet asserted themselves, that state in which each person was individually and narcissistically self-sufficient. This sexual wish-state is that of androgyny—everyone an hermaphrodite, a perfect balance of sexes. Such androgynes need no others to experience fulfillment; they are able to exist in a state of permanent innocence and self-sufficiency.

This androgynous state is greatly desired by Miss L, but he must reject Betty's way of achieving it because of her retreat from life. He wants to advance into existence, accepting the dualities of life and finding a unity in diversity. Retreat from the unpleasant side of things, or rejection of it, smacks of self-love and self-defeat; his answer must be selfless.

In visions he finds this solution in Christ and the doctrine of *agape*, the selfless love of acceptance. In Christ he finds not a retreat from life to former innocence, but rather a reinstatement of innocence on Man by Christ's redemptive presence. He feels in the power of Jesus the enforcement of harmony in the midst of diversity—the making of life into a whole of conflicting parts by the acceptance of order in divinity. It is the vision of Jesus given in Galatians: "There is neither Jew nor Greek, there is neither bond nor free, there is neither male nor female; for ye are all one in Christ Jesus" (3:28). The harmonization of discordant forces, the reinstatement of androgynous innocence, occurs not in the deceptive simplicity of any verdant Eden, but on barren Calvary hill.

In the transport of a "fever" in the solitude of his room after administering the Eucharist to himself with crackers and water (84), Jesus comes alive as Miss L stares at his impaled figure. Jesus becomes a bright fly, the world, a leaping fish which consumes the fly and is ennobled by it by exuding a bright beauty and a splash of music. All else in the room seems dead next to this image; Christ becomes the totality of "life and light" (93). At this point head and heart and innocence and fruition all come together: "He felt clean and fresh. His heart was a rose and in his skull another rose bloomed" (93).

The roses are the result of his cultivation of the "garden of his mind," and he has become the new Androgynes in the garden-state. He is able to formulate a plan of action based on his new acceptance of divine order, in which all of his columns will be submitted to God. But the vision is a fleeting one. He is immediately confronted with his other self, crippled Peter, who has come to kill him. In his first gesture of love under this new plan, he goes to embrace Peter, is misunderstood, and is accidentally shot. As someone has observed earlier in the book, it is very difficult "to find a market for the fruits of . . . personality," for the flowers of even the most effectively cultivated "interior garden." The response to an act of love is the same as that to any other stimulus, absurd destruction and death.

An Illiberal Education:
William Golding's Pedagogy

▉▉▉▉▉▉▉▉▉▉▉▉▉

George Clark

In *Lord of the Flies* and *Pincher Martin,* William Golding drama-tizes a process which leads inexorably toward an aphorism on mankind.[1] Golding engages protagonist and reader in this process of enlightenment and takes a schoolmasterly tone with both protagonist and reader. In *Lord of the Flies* Golding's pedagogical bent has prompted the choice of a child, a boy of twelve, as protagonist. At the close of both novels an unexpected ending, an ending presenting a surprising turn of events or startling shift in point of view, forces the audience to "rethink the book, which seems to me a useful thing to do."[2] The protagonist, on his part, is forced to rethink the experience and recognize the truth it embodied, the aphorism toward which the work was aimed. The protagonist's recognition, and the reader's, are sudden and astounding in impact, but thoroughly prepared for in the protagonist's experience and almost grasped before. The final perception is to be at once surprising and familiar, a sudden rising to consciousness of what was subliminally known; at the moment of truth, the reader and the protagonist are supposed, as it were, to supply something like—"oh yes! that's it, and I had it on the tip of my tongue too!" If the aphorism aimed at in *Lord of the Flies* is, as Golding put it, "an attempt to trace the defects of society back to the defects of human nature,"[3] the aphorism *Pincher Martin* develops would trace the defects of the individual to a passionate attachment to personal survival, preservation of identity, constant assertion of self "at all costs" to use Christopher Martin's own words.

[1] The editions cited are the soft-cover Capricorn Books (New York: G. P. Putnam's Sons); *Lord of the Flies* is dated 1959 (first published 1954), *Pincher Martin* bears only the original copyright date, 1956.

[2] One of Golding's contributions to the "Purdue Interview" (May 10, 1962).

[3] Quoted in E. L. Epstein's notes appended to *Lord of the Flies*, p. 189.

Since *Lord of the Flies* has often been publicly analyzed as illustrating a process of man's moral corruption—more accurately, a
progressive revelation of man's moral corruption—I should like to
examine the book as illustrating the process of enlightenment, and
to follow the protagonist's education in the Goldinesque philosophy.
This emphasis has one disadvantage for *Lord of the Flies*: Ralph is
a good, dull boy; and a corresponding advantage for *Pincher Martin*: Chris is a fascinating hero, a real four-letter man. This proce-
dure highlights a weakness in *Lord of the Flies*; despite Golding's
intention, the novel might prompt us to see the "defects of society"
arising from individual villains rather than the "defects of human
nature."

The protagonist of *Lord of the Flies*, a fair-haired boy known only
as Ralph, undergoes a spiritual and intellectual development of a
familiar pattern; he begins in idyllic and innocent and empty-
headed detachment, moves to a public-spirited though deluded optimism, finds himself becoming disillusioned and spiritually indifferent, discovers disillusionment turning into despair and bafflement, and at last reaches a tragic, but, in Golding's terms, clear
perception of the innate wickedness of mankind, a view the reader
is strongly invited to endorse. It is the darkness of man's heart, not
the moral disintegration of a few boys, that Ralph perceives at the
end of *Lord of the Flies*. The mechanism of Ralph's enlightenment
is his involvement in a struggle against external and internal im-
pulses toward violence, destruction, and savagery even without fully
understanding them. As far as the external action is concerned,
Ralph struggles in a losing cause, and his tragic vision is the product
of defeat in the realm of external action.

The setting of *Lord of the Flies* excites in Ralph, in the children
generally, and in the reader pastoral expectations that the narrator
intends to disappoint, in the midst of an atomic war, the children
reach a tropical island which seems, like Arcady or Arden, detached
from the heartaches and disorders of the outer world. On the island,
the children find flower and fruit on the same tree, fresh water, a

lagoon which shields them from knowledge of the profound and measureless extent of the surrounding Pacific.

If we "rethink the book" as we go along, its opening scenes ironically counterpoint the idyllic motif. The first words of the novel direct our attention toward the attractive Ralph: "The boy with the fair hair . . ." and a little later Ralph is again "The fair boy . . ." Ralph, a pleasing figure of innocence, resonates to the tropical beauty of the place: "He . . . stood looking down into the water. It was clear to the bottom and bright with the efflorescence of tropical weed and coral. A school of tiny, glittering fish flicked hither and thither. Ralph spoke to himself, sounding the bass strings of delight. 'Whizzoh!' " Thereafter: "Beyond the platform there was more enchantment. Some act of God—a typhoon perhaps, or the storm that had accompanied his own arrival—had banked sand inside the lagoon so that there was a long, deep pool in the beach with a high ledge of pink granite at the further end. . . . the incredible pool, which clearly was only invaded by the sea at high tide, was so deep at one end as to be dark green. The water was warmer than his blood and he might have been swimming in a huge bath."

The passage overtly concentrates attention on the harmony between the fair boy and lush nature, but the references to storm, typhoon, and blood oppose that idyllic vision; moreover, Ralph makes his way to "the incredible pool" by following a "long scar smashed into the jungle" and strips for his swim "among the skull-like coconuts." And though Ralph delights in the beauty of the pool, the narrator has, at the very outset of the novel, placed him in an alien context: "The fair boy stopped and jerked his stockings with an automatic gesture that made the jungle seem for a moment like the Home Counties." The sentence which begins so matter-of-factly ends with a foreboding juxtaposition of the "Home Counties," those urban and urbane counties nearest London, the British version of the area east of the Hudson River, and "the jungle." The "jungle" and the "Home Counties" are at the antipodes; Ralph does not know this, but the fat boy for whom he briefly stops voices the anxiety which the narrator has suggested. On learning that "Perhaps there aren't any grownups anywhere," the fat boy is startled, and his reaction is ominous. He hurries after Ralph: "Aren't there any grownups at all?" Ralph stands on his head. While Ralph swims with expert ease—his harmony with nature again—Piggy, who cannot swim at all, questions Ralph's calm assurance. Casually, Ralph voices his faith; his father will get leave and then "he'll come and rescue us." Piggy asks some home questions: "When'll your dad rescue us?" "Soon as he can." And then, over the roar of the breakers beating on the reef out beyond the calm pool, Piggy asks "How does he know we're here?" Getting no answer, he asks again "How does he know we're here?" Having established their isolation, Piggy tearfully concludes "We may stay here till we die." The narrator observes: "With that word the heat seemed to increase till it became a threatening weight and the lagoon attacked them with a blinding effulgence." Ralph crosses the sand "enduring the sun's enmity" and finds that "To put on a grey shirt once more was strangely pleasing." Nature and human nakedness are not on the terms Ralph supposes.

The process of Ralph's enlightenment begins when Piggy succeeds in prompting the dreaming, fair boy into participation in an attempt to establish a human order on the island, an order based on rationality and aimed at rescue; Piggy repeatedly insists: "We got to do something." The instrument and symbol of that order is the conch; Ralph sees it first and points into the lagoon: "Something creamy lay among the ferny weeds." Ralph's successful efforts to fish the conch out of the water are sandwiched between Piggy's excited reactions to it: "I seen one like that before. On someone's back wall. A conch he called it." The beautiful shell appeals to Piggy because it provides a tangible point of reference for his memories of a benevolent civilization; he remembers his friend "used to blow it and then his mum would come." Piggy babbles of the conch's value: "It's ever so valuable" and then "ever so expensive. I bet if you wanted to buy one, you'd have to pay pounds and pounds and pounds." Piggy's commercial instinct, ludicrously out of place here, illustrates his thoroughgoing commitment to the values and the systems of evaluation of normal, civilized, adult humanity. Ralph sees the conch with a child's eyes: "The shell was interesting and pretty and a worthy plaything; but the vivid phantoms of his daydream still interposed between him and Piggy, who in this context was an irrelevance." Inspiration hits Piggy with a flash of brilliance, "Ralph! . . . We can use this to call the others. Have a meeting. They'll come when they hear us—" and then, "That was what you meant, didn't you? That's why you got the conch out of the water?" Whether or not Piggy believes it, that ascription of adult purpose to an essentially childlike action sets Ralph's foot on the path of involvement, responsibility, and, ultimately, understanding. When Ralph learns how to sound the conch its deep harsh note reverberates across the island, frightens birds and a pig; the boy is transformed: "His ordinary voice sounded like a whisper after the harsh note of the conch." He sounds it again: ". . . birds cried, small animals scuttered." The sound of the conch sets Ralph and the nature he luxuriated in at odds: "The conch was silent, a gleaming tusk; Ralph's face was dark with breathlessness and the air over the island was full of bird-clamor and echoes ringing." The "gleaming tusk" suggests, I think, Roland's horn, the Oliphant, so-called because it was made from an elephant's tusk; the allusion to Roland's horn is ominous, it was a betrayed and dying Roland who sounded the Oliphant at Roncesvalles; nevertheless, the allusion ennobles Ralph.

The other children begin to appear and accept the authority assumed by Ralph and Piggy as the fat boy goes through the crowd asking names: "The children gave him the same simple obedience that they had given the men with the megaphones." The conch (nature) has taken the place of the megaphone (artifice) as the symbol of authority. Piggy's first question to Ralph, we might recall, was "Where's the man with the megaphone?" Sounding the conch, the first step in attempting to bring order to the island and by implication an assumption of authority, brings about the first con-

frontation between Ralph and Jack, the ugly, red-haired choir-
leader who leaps, cloak flying, onto the platform and, blinded by
the sun, asks "Where's the man with the trumpet?" Jack's identification of the sound of the shell as a trumpet's blast arises from
the instrument's martial origin and connections. In spite of Jack's
charisma and Piggy's intelligence, the children choose Ralph for
their chief: ". . . there was a stillness about Ralph as he sat that
marked him out: there was his size, and attractive appearance; and
most obscurely, yet most powerfully, there was the conch. The being
that had blown that, had sat waiting for them on the platform with
the delicate thing balanced on his knees, was set apart. 'Him with
the shell.' 'Ralph, Ralph!' 'Let him be chief with the trumpet-thing'."
The ambiguity of the last sentence is crucial; it is the boy with the
"trumpet-thing" who is to be chief and it is by means of the "trumpet-thing" that he is chief. Even Jack admits the conch's authority;
". . . your shell called us." The shell becomes the visible token of
the island's constitution; like the herald's staff in Homer, the conch
symbolizes the speaker's right to the attention of the assembly, it
becomes the focal point of parliamentary democracy.

In the public-spirited optimism of Ralph's first assembly as chief,
he proposes two goals for island existence: to be rescued and to have
fun. Both social aims seem possible because, as Jack, Ralph, and
Simon report after exploring it, "this is a good island." Ralph's disillusionment and lethargy stem from a growing sense that "good
island" or not, not all is well and that the two aims of having fun
and getting rescued are opposed; after the first disaster on the island
—an uncontrolled signal fire which evidently burns up one of the
"littluns"—Piggy had warned that to be rescued they must "put
first things first and act proper." Ralph clashes with Jack over what
things must be first—hunting (the new definition of fun) or the
signal fire; meat or shelters. Ralph insists that "The best thing we
can do is get ourselves rescued" and the narrator observes that "Jack
had to think a moment before he could remember what rescue was."
Jack's answer recalls Piggy's dictum: "Rescue? Yes, of course! All

the same, I'd like to catch a pig first." The two boys mock one another's version of the highest good—"You and your fire!" and "All
you can talk about is pig, pig, pig!" Thereafter Jack strips the fire-
detail and manages to kill his first pig; all the boys meet at the top
of the mountain—the signal fire has gone out, a ship is just passing
out of sight, and the values of fire and pig have clashed head on.

Disheartened, Ralph calls an assembly, where he will make a
carefully considered attempt to reassert the order and the optimism
with which they began. However, "happiness" rather than "fun"
is now Ralph's secondary social goal and the difference suggests an
increased rationality and moderated hope. As he plans the assembly
Ralph views himself and his immediate past with a detachment,
honesty, and irony essential to the boy's final grasp of man's plight;
Ralph reflects that the assembly "must not be fun, but business,"
and he realizes without envy that "I can't think. Not like Piggy."
Ralph smiles jeeringly at the memory of the first enthusiastic ex-
ploration of the island, and so rejects, perhaps unconsciously, the
relevance of that pastoral report, "this is a good island." Presided
over by Ralph and sanctified by the conch, the gathering begins as
a parliamentary assembly "to put things straight" and re-establish
an endangered social order; at the end of his speech Ralph confesses
his disillusionment and perplexity: "Things are breaking up. I don't
understand why. We began well; we were happy. And then—"
The gathering ends in a barbaric dance led by Jack. Ralph despairs:
"I ought to give up being chief." Piggy is horrified: "If Jack was
chief, he'd have all hunting and no fire. We'd be here till we died."
Simon agrees: "Piggy's right, Ralph. There's you and Jack. Keep
on being chief."

That night the body of an airman, slain in a battle ten miles up,
lands on the island near the signal fire; the parachute tugs at it and
the body moves with the breezes. The airman's dead body, accepted
as "the beast," catalyzes the fear which has slowly grown up in the
island society; that fear first found its external justification in a
"snake-thing" or "beastie" dreamed of by the "littlun" lost in the

fire. The "beastie" later took more definite shape as "a thing, a dark thing, a beast, some sort of animal" felt especially by the hunters. In the form of the dead airman, the beast takes Jack's side in the conflict between hunting and rescue. Ralph complains: "And now that thing squats by the fire as though it didn't want us to be rescued. . . . We're beaten." After some gruesome doings, Jack's hunters form a tribe under his chieftainship. To be independent Jack must have Piggy's fire-making spectacles—for cooking fires. With two hunters Jack slips to the shelter where the others are asleep. Ralph and Piggy hear something outside in the darkness and quietly panic: "Desperately Ralph prayed that the beast would prefer littluns." Outside, Jack deliberately accepts his role as the beast: "A voice whispered horribly outside. 'Piggy—Piggy—' 'It's come!' gasped Piggy. 'It's real!' " The voice continues: "Piggy, come outside. I want you Piggy." We should recall that when Jack and the choir first answered the sound of the shell they were seen as "something dark" and then as "the creature."

At first the discovery that the beast outside was Jack and his hunters merely deepens Ralph's bafflement and numbed anguish: ". . . the signal's out and we can't ever be rescued." Piggy plans an appeal to the authority of conch; holding it he will demand his spectacles back "because what's right's right." As they plan Ralph can only remember that somehow smoke is terribly important; Piggy must remind him why. Ralph's bafflement is essential to his final vision of man's nature; shattering experience has left him no room for any other view of humanity, but he cannot yet formulate that final statement on mankind; he needs the impetus of horror and a moment to step back and see the whole experience in perspective. The attempt to regain Piggy's spectacles ends in Piggy's death as Roger, "with a sense of delirious abandonment," launches a huge rock against the helpless boy and fragile conch—both are destroyed in an instant. At once Jack leaps forward: "I meant that!" And the tribe pursues Ralph like a hunted pig. Escaping, Ralph finds a pig's skull stuck up on the end of a spear; it is now as white and gleaming as was the conch, a symbol of the island's new constitution, and the skull indeed of the Lord of the Flies. After contemplating that pig's head on a stick, Simon had reached his perception of the human condition; as "the beast" the pig's head had spoken to Simon saying, "You knew, didn't you? I'm part of you? Close, close, close! I'm the reason why it's no go? Why things are what they are?" Ralph dislodges the skull and takes the spear; if the pig's head spoke to Simon, the stake that held it up eventually becomes Ralph's guide to why "things are what they are."

Slipping back to Jack's stronghold, Ralph finds the captured twins are now part of the tribe and asks them, "But what are you going to do when you catch me?" And getting no answer he asks again, "What are you going to do—?" The reluctant answer adds to Ralph's bafflement: "Roger sharpened a stick at both ends." Hiding for the night, Ralph puzzles over the mystery—"What did it mean? A stick sharpened at both ends. What was there in that?" Burnt out of his lair, Ralph races through the forest trying to think what should be done, whether to climb a tree, burst through the thin line of hunters sweeping across the island, or to hide and hope they would pass by him. Hiding—with two chances instead of one—Ralph puzzles once more—"A stick sharpened at both ends." With the whole forest on fire and a savage approaching, Ralph "fumbled to hold his spear so that it was point foremost; and now he saw that the stick was sharpened at both ends." Screaming at the horror, Ralph breaks through the line of hunters, races through the forest to the beach, falls crying for mercy, and staggers to his feet to be greeted by a naval officer who says "Hullo." The island's smoke has brought a ship and rescue to the children; Ralph remembers the "strange glamour that had once invested the beaches" and remembers Simon's death—and Jack. No longer baffled, Ralph weeps "for the end of innocence, the darkness of man's heart, and the fall through the air of the true wise friend called Piggy." The innocence that has ended is Ralph's ignorance of mankind's essential illness. The unexpected rescue, the trick ending of the novel as some have put it, re-establishes the distance between the audience and Ralph who, as the naval officer observes, is a "little scarecrow" in need of "a bath, a haircut, a nose-wipe and a good deal of ointment." Unexpectedly we can see Ralph in perspective, the perspective of a world at war. When Ralph looks up at his rescuer he sees a uniform —from the top of the peaked cap to the row of gilt buttons—and a revolver; there's no face. The narrator observes, "The officer looked at Ralph doubtfully for a moment, then took his hand away from the butt of the revolver." Behind the officer is his boat and in it an enlisted man is holding a submachine gun; offshore the "trim cruiser," a warship momentarily at peace, awaits the rescued boys. Ralph's final perception of the force that broke things up on the island, the darkness of man's heart, holds good for the world of adult, atomic war with which the novel begins and ends.

While one hardly needs to summarize the plot of *Lord of the Flies*, he can hardly retell the story of *Pincher Martin*. Pincher, I might point out now, is the man's nickname, the nickname given almost all men named Martin in the British navy. I shall call the man Chris, as do his friends and enemies—rather more of the latter than the former—in civilian life. *Pincher Martin* begins with a man struggling desperately in the water and yelling profanely for help. The man manages to float just at the surface, remembers who he is and what he should do: he sets about the techniques of survival at sea; first he maneuvers to discard his seaboots, then he blows up his life-preserver. He struggles to see if there are other survivors, if there is any wreckage about from his ship. The swimmer's ship has evidently been torpedoed shortly before dawn; soon after light begins to return, Chris Martin sees something in the water; he yells and swims frantically, then realizes it is a rock. Chris reaches the rock and most of the rest of the book is ostensibly concerned with his heroic efforts to survive—to signal for rescue—and his recurring memories of his past life. The efforts at survival seem heroic; the memories of the past, however, recreate a character whose loss almost no one would regret. Along with the struggle for food and shelter, Chris must contend against sickness of the body and delirium of the mind, although in the last stages of his stay on the great rock he courts insanity and at last talks with an apparent hallucination, a figure dressed in a sailor's outfit and wearing seaboots; the visitant is usually taken to be God and Chris accepts him as God—and Chris defies both God and heaven. The visitant disappears and Chris tries to rave as the sea, rock, and all disappear into an absolute nothingness shattered and annihilated by the tendrils of a black lightning; at last nothing is left but the center of Chris's consciousness and his hands, now red claws, locked together. The black lightning plays over the claws and waits to pierce the center. The book's last, brief chapter brings two new characters into the story: Campbell, a native of the outer Hebrides, and Davidson, a naval officer on a kind of rescue mission. Campbell has acquired an unwanted dead body, the corrupted corpse of a sailor washed up on the beach. After Davidson checks the body's identity disc, Campbell asks out of the horror and pathos of the experience: "You know nothing of my—shall I say—official beliefs, Mr. Davidson; but living for all these days next to that poor derelict—Mr. Davidson. Would you say there was any—surviving? Or is that all?" Davidson cannot understand the question, and asks "If you're worried about Martin—whether he suffered or not—" and Campbell, defeated, lets that stand for his question, for Davidson *can* answer that, and does: "Then don't worry about him. You saw the body. He didn't even have time to kick off his seaboots."

If Chris didn't have time to kick off his seaboots, we must agree with Golding that rethinking the book is indeed "a useful thing to do." But before plunging into an examination of *Pincher Martin*, we may look briefly at its narrative technique. In the water and on the rock, Chris is visited by memories of his past life as snapshots or stills, brief and isolated scenes—sometimes with sound—and as film-trailers or previews, short runs like sections of a movie, always with sound and astonishingly realistic. Chris finds himself in them rather than recalling them in his memory—the first time he notices that, he's rather upset about the realism. He tells himself, "I was asleep then. I was dreaming." The snapshots and the film-trailers (Chris uses both words himself) are closely connected; most of the film-trailers are in fact previewed by a snapshot. Chris has reflections and memories of the more normal sort as well, but he seems to have no control over the scheduling of his movies or of the snapshots. Chris never allows himself to ask who is the manager of the theatre or why it's running on the barren rock. Chris's last film-trailer brings him just up to the point where we found him at the outset of the novel, his struggle with the "black impervious water," and the fact of the symmetry is significant, as is the symmetry itself. A number of recurring motifs appear in the snapshots, the film-trailers, and Chris's rock-bound reflections: the most important of these are teeth (and eating), around which Chris reconstructs the appalling philosophy by which he has lived, a Chinese box for which he searches in his memory and which he finds at last—and also a looted metal cashbox associated with the first partly because it is japanned, a woman, Mary Lovell, and a man, Nathaniel Walterson, and George, Pete, and Helen, the director, producer, and producer's wife most intimately connected with Chris's professional career as an actor.

But what about the seaboots, abandoned according to good survival technique on the second page of the novel, and thereafter frequently lamented by Chris who wishes that he had them back again, and which turn up on his rotten corpse, Campbell's unwanted guest? Between the fact of the seaboots and the discussions of death and dying which form part of Chris's film-trailers—his memories of his friend Nathaniel Walterson—it is clear that Chris drowns on the second page of the novel, that his tremendous drive for survival, for the preservation of his identity, forces him to create for himself the false appearance of a life which is in fact his purgatory. Golding, a cooperative author, has confirmed this view of the basic fable of

Pincher Martin.[4] The novel is part of a very large body of man-overboard and man-marooned literature (one thinks of *Robinson Crusoe* and "The Castaway"), but if we look over the highpoints of Chris's story—death by water, survival on a rock, the rock's destruction, defiance of God, insistence of personal survival, the will of God or of the sea notwithstanding—one may guess that Golding's narrative has been influenced by the oldest version of the death-at-sea theme in western literature: the account of the death of Aias in Book IV of Homer's *Odyssey.*[5] In the passage I shall quote, Menelaus reports to Telemachus, Odysseus' son, some news about the leaders of the Trojan expedition which Menelaus was able to obtain from the Old Man of the Sea (Menelaus quotes the Old Man verbatim of course):

Aias, to take him first, was wrecked in his long-oared galleys by Poseidon, who drove him onto the great cliff of Gyrae and then rescued him from the surf. In fact, he would have evaded his doom, in spite of Athene's enmity, if in his blind folly he had not talked so big, boasting that he had escaped from the hungry jaws of the sea in defiance of the gods. His loud-voiced blasphemy came to the ears of Poseidon, who seized his trident in his powerful hands, struck the Gyraean rock and split it into two. One half stood firm, but the fragment he had severed, where Aias had been resting when the mad impulse took him, crashed into the sea and carried him with it into the vast and rolling depths, where he gulped the salt water down and perished.

We can hardly doubt that Golding had this section of Book IV in mind when he wrote *Pincher Martin,* because at one point Chris sees a number of seals playing around the three rocks near his refuge, thinks of killing one for the sake of meat and sealskin boots, and then reflects: "The men lay on the open beach, wrapped in skins. They endured the long wait and the stench. At dusk, the great beasts came out of the sea, played around them, then lay down to sleep." With some minor inaccuracies and omissions (Chris fre-

[4] Quoted by Samuel Hynes, *William Golding* (New York: Columbia University Press, 1964), pp. 27–28.
[5] Translation by E. V. Rieu (Baltimore: Penguin Books, 1946).

quently misquotes literary texts), this paraphrases Menelaus'
description of the trick he used to capture the Old Man of the Sea.
Once caught, the Old Man revealed what had happened to the other
heroes of the war, Agamemnon, Odysseus, and Aias. Just before his
interview with the visitant dressed as a sailor and accepted as God,
Chris identifies himself with Prometheus, who also suffered on a
rock because of the enmity of a god armed with lightning and in
the same breath with Ajax, that is, Aias. That belated identification
is part of Chris's conscious admission and acceptance of the truth
that he is dead and must now surrender that hoarded and enjoyed
identity whose constant assertion has been his one goal; an ex-actor
and a true ham, Chris has consistently seen himself as first one and
then another literary hero—Hamlet and Lear for instances. But I
think that he has most consistently seen himself as Odysseus, the
man who survived war and shipwreck and came through alive to
live the "damned long life" Chris has wanted and predicted for himself. At one point his friend Nat had remarked "you have an
extraordinary capacity to endure" and Chris remembers the remark
with pleasure—we may recall that Homer repeatedly speaks of
Odysseus as "long-suffering" and "much-enduring." Odysseus too
is the man supremely gifted with "mother-wit" and a "man of
many wiles;" Chris repeatedly characterizes himself as "brilliantly
clever" and the film-trailers of his past show clearly enough that
he has been a man of many petty wiles. This representation of
Chris as a man who sees himself as Odysseus but whose story follows the shape of the misfortunes of Aias, the knucklehead who
doomed himself by his own folly, illustrates the irony in Golding's
conception of his protagonist.

Chris Martin's "ravenous ego"—to use Golding's own expression
—drives him to create the illusion of a rock and the illusion of a
life on the rock, but he finally concedes the unreality of the rock
and the life.[6] Chris concedes because he is forced to admit conscious-

---

[6] Hynes, *William Golding*, p. 27.

ly that his life on the rock has not been real, that the experience is full of holes, that there are clear traces of unreality all around. The final recognition which brings Chris to the unwelcome conclusion that he's dead is his realization that the rock duplicates a molar he had extracted long ago; its shape is branded on his consciousness by pain. This reluctant discovery raises some intriguing questions: If Chris invents the world he lives in, why does he invent the painful experience on the rock? Couldn't a free and ravenous ego invent something more gratifying? And if Chris does invent it, why does he see its imperfections and discover its unreality from those imperfections? I think that we must at first conclude that Chris's ego is not free to invent any form of survival. Something external to Chris apparently directs the selection and sequence of the film-trailers which reconstruct his life, character, and philosophy, and that same something external to Chris establishes the terms of his illusory survival. Since Golding has avowed a religious purpose in the novel, we may believe that Chris Martin's experience on the rock is a purgatorial experience inflicted by the God who appears as a sailor and asks Chris "Have you had enough, Christopher?" But Chris himself admits—or the "dark centre" of his being admits—the unreality of his survival, and thus consents to his annihilation. Safe on his rock, Chris had looked at the "quiet sea" and declared: "I don't claim to be a hero. But I've got health and education and intelligence. I'll beat you." These are the terms of his "determination to survive," thus when intelligence and education begin to find flaws in his survival, Chris is logically committed to nonsurvival. But Chris's surrender to "reason and truth" and death suggests that within "the dark centre of his being" a dramatic conflict takes place between an impulse toward self-deception and survival, on the one hand, and an impulse toward recognition of the truth and annihilation, on the other.

In *Pincher Martin* the dramatic conflict at the heart of the book's educational process is submerged below the conscious level of Chris's "dark centre," but the tremors from that struggle are perceptible very early in the book. When Chris reaches the foot of his rock—it is cleft at the bottom but the two parts join above his head —"He made quacking sounds with his mouth. The words that had formed in his mind were: Where is this bloody rock? But that seemed to risk something by insult of the dark cleft so that he changed them in his throat. 'Where the hell am I?' " Contemplating the rock unaccountably thrust into "the inconceivable vastness of the whole ocean," Chris panics: "An evil pervasion, not the convulsive panic of his first struggles in the water, but a deep and generalized terror set him clawing at the rock with his blunt fingers." In short, something down there doesn't believe in the existence of the rock, says it's a fake, and Chris claws at it to assure himself of the rock's reality. But that isn't enough; if the rock deceives the sight, it can deceive the touch as well, and Chris admonishes himself desperately: "Think, you bloody fool, think." And while Chris gropes in his memory for confirmation of the rock's existence, the sea seems to threaten him and the pebbles he stands on seem to tremble: "The horizon of misty water stayed close, the water leapt from the rock and the pebbles wavered. 'Think'." Those who have paddled in the waves at the seashore will recall the optical illusion by which pebbles seem to waver or move as the depth of the water over them changes, but Chris's pebbles waver, we now know, like the flame of a candle in a draft. Chris finds the memory that momentarily saves him from truth: "The spark was alight and the heart was supplying it with what it wanted." He remembers the captain of a cruiser, its navigating commander, himself as the navigator's yeoman, and the chart: "That name was written on the chart, well out in the Atlantic, eccentrically isolated. . . . The captain spoke with his clipped Dartmouth accent—spoke and laughed. 'I call that name a near miss'."

The crisis passed, Chris denies it existed: "I am no better off than I was." The captain calls the name a near miss because the name of the rock, the name which Chris can never quite remember, almost rhymes with a British obscenity meaning "nothing." The expression isn't used in the states, but it consists merely of adding-*all* to a well-established obscenity, one of the four-letter words, *the* four-letter word I might say. It doesn't rhyme exactly with British "rock," but, as the captain says, it's a near miss. If the characterization of Chris as a four-letter man is apt—Golding remarks that Chris is fallen man and adds "in fact he's a good deal more fallen than most"[7]— we must wonder that he should forget the rhyme that made the Dartmouth captain laugh. The explanation is, I think, that Chris suppresses his memory of the rock's *name* because even if he were alive on Rockall, he would be doomed: Rockall rises out of a sand-bank which extends twenty-five by fifty miles; it was not sighted until 1810, and it is not often sighted since ships do not often venture within the fifteen or so miles that Chris estimates he could be seen from; and even if a ship sighted the rock and Chris's signal, a dwarf of heaped-up stones made to resemble a man, no ship could stand by in wartime while a small boat crossed the shallows to the rock—but Chris's destroyer would never have come close enough to Rockall for him to be washed up on it after a few hours in the water.

At many other points we may detect Chris suppressing, ignoring, and turning away from unmistakable clues to the rock's unreality and his own death. The awareness of the fact of his death is always just below the surface of his consciousness and the admission slips out at odd and unguarded moments; for example, even as he first climbs up the rock from its dark cleft, Chris is surprised at the un-wieldiness of his flesh and blurts out "Like a dead man!" Later, when the consciousness of death has begun to haunt him, Chris feels his cheeks and reflects "I must have a beard pretty well. Bristles, any-way. Strange that bristles go on growing even when the rest of you is—" Chris cuts that consideration off most abruptly: "He went quickly off to Prospect cliff . . ." Only a little earlier he had looked at the scene before him "and it was a picture. He shut his eyes and

---

[7] Quoted by John Bowen, "Bending over Backwards," *Times Literary Supplement* (October 23, 1959), p. 608.

then opened them again but the rock and the sea seemed no more real."

If, as I have suggested, the place and circumstances of Chris's purgatorial experience, even including the selection and arrangement of his movies, are forced upon him from outside, Golding's assertion that he followed a rigidly marked-out program for this novel holds up very well indeed.[8] But if the purgatorial experience on the rock is as basically pedagogical as Ralph's experience on the island, the problem is to locate the object of the pedagogy, and I do not believe—despite one or two misguided reviewers—that the object is a *mea culpa* and repentance on Chris's part; if the essential stuff of the narrative is the submerged struggle between self-deception and enlightenment, as I maintain it is, the discovery that Chris is "a good deal more fallen" than most of mankind is hardly the novel's point. Moreover, I can see only slight traces of remorse in Chris Martin's memories of his past life. We do discover, to be sure, that Chris has experimented with pederasty, indulged in adultery, attempted something rather like rape, emptied a cash-box, intended an indirect murder just when the torpedo hit, and, worst of all, cheated in his examinations: one of his snapshot memories is of a very small French dictionary which looks just like a very large eraser—and *now* we know how Chris passed his Oxford matriculation examination in French!

One of the film-trailers of memory imposed upon Chris Martin's consciousness represents a conventionally religious conception of his character. This particular movie of Chris's past was previewed by a snapshot memory when he first reached the rock. Chris relives in it a rather harrowing experience: George and Pete, the director-actor and producer, choose a second part for Chris in an impending production—everyone's doubling but naturally Chris protests. Chris is to double as one of the seven deadly sins, and the discussion takes place backstage where seven painted masks, each representing one

[8] Quoted by Frank Kermode, "The Novels of William Golding," *International Literary Annual*, III (1961), 11.

of the sins, await their actors. A three-way discussion follows as to which mask would best become Chris. The "Helen" mentioned in the discussion is Pete's wife. Chris's high-road to the theatre has lain directly through Helen—as Pete evidently has begun to realize. I shall begin with Pete's opening remark when the three men first look over the masks:

"What about Pride, George? He could play that without a mask and just stylized make-up couldn't he?"

"Look, Pete, if I'm doubling I'd rather not make—"

"Malice, George?"

"Envy, Pete?"

"I don't mind playing Sloth, Pete."

"Not Sloth. Shall we ask Helen, Chris? I value my wife's advice."

"Steady, Pete."

"What about a spot of Lechery?"

"Pete! Stop it!"

"Don't mind me, Chris, old man. I'm just a bit wrought-up, that's all. Now here's a fine piece of work, ladies and gentlemen, guaranteed unworn. Any offers? Going to the smooth-looking gentleman with the wavy hair and profile. Going! Going—"

"What's it supposed to be, old man?"

"Darling, it's simply *you*! Don't you think, George?"

"Definitely, old man, definitely."

"Chris-Greed. Greed-Chris. Know each other."

"Anything to please you, Pete."

"Let me make you two better acquainted. This painted bastard here takes anything he can lay his hands on. Not food, Chris, that's far too simple. He takes the best part, the best seat, the most money, the best notice, the best woman. He was born with his mouth and his flies open and both hands out to grab. He's a cosmic case of the bugger who gets his penny and someone else's bun. Isn't that right, George?"

"Come on, Pete. Come and lie down for a bit."

"Think you can play Martin, Greed?"

Pete's shot "Think you can play Martin, Greed?" applies to Chris the characterization of "this painted bastard here"—the mask of

Greed—and the reversal makes the man, Chris Martin, later nick-named Pincher, the archetype of the sin. The orthodox religious conception of Chris's character and past is external; it is based on his behavior, his behavior is not based on it. On the rock, as Chris's consciously controlled memories and thoughts contemplate the stuff of the involuntary replays of his past, he first articulates the philoso-phy which has shaped his life and his view of life; it is a philosophy of eating—"eating women, eating men, crunching up Alfred, that other girl, that boy . . ." and its objective symbol, appropriately and ironically, is—teeth. His creed formulated, Chris searches for its genesis. Chris repeatedly contemplates, as a clue to his condition, a childhood memory, the memory of a terrifying darkness he imag-ined to be in the cellar and toward which he, in fantasy, was horri-fyingly drawn. He associated that darkness with the ends of coffins protruding from the cellar wall, with decay and violent death. That darkness apparently represents the absolute blackness of nonbeing from which Chris knows he has come. With his defenses against the knowledge of death falling all about him, Chris plays at being mad, pretends to give the darkness of the cellar an external form, that of an old woman, and attacks her—his oilskin that is—with his knife: "He shouted at the rocks but the old woman would not appear among them. She had slipped away down to the cellar. Then he glimpsed her lying huddled in the crevice and he struggled up to her. He fell on her and began to slash with his knife while his mouth went on shouting. 'That'll teach you to chase me! That'll teach you to chase me out of the cellar through cars and beds and pubs, you at the back and me running, running after my identity disc all the days of my life! Bleed and die'." The clue is the identity disc; the first thing Chris Martin did when safely on the rock was to undress, look himself over, look at his identity disc, and search for his papers with the attached photograph of himself. When he feels his grasp on his identity slipping Chris recalls that he was a man with twenty photographs of himself; he defines the pleasure he had in sex: it lay in the definition of his body, the gratification of his sense of being.

The experience which Chris Martin does not control, his illusory rock and realistic movies, forces him to his own analysis of his condition both past and present. Chris doesn't repent his individual sins and crimes; he becomes aware of their ultimate source in "his ravenous ego." Chris Martin's beast was that insatiable hunger to assert his isolated being.

If we look once more at novelist Golding as a pedagogue, we might say that Ralph is educated by the elective system—he elects to sound the conch and the boys elect him chief—and graduates when he learns "to trace the defects of society back to the defects of human nature." Chris Martin, nicknamed Pincher and christened Christopher, the Christ-bearer, follows a prescribed course of study and graduates when he learns that the defects of the individual are traceable to the assertion of selfhood "at all costs." Both the man and the boy engage in a losing struggle to maintain an order based on an illusion, and by admitting defeat attain truth.

From Here to Absurdity:
Heller's **Catch-22**

Vance Ramsey

Catch-22, published in 1961, was greeted by extremely mixed reviews. Reactions ranged all the way from frank adulation to contemptuous dismissal. Nelson Algren said of it, "To compare *Catch-22* favorably with *The Good Soldier Schweik* would be an injustice, because this novel is not merely the best American novel to come out of World War II; it is the best American novel that has come out of anywhere in years."[1] Julian Mitchell, writing in *Spectator*, called it "a book of enormous richness and art, of deep thought and brilliant writing."[2] On the other side are those like Whitney Balliett in his review in *The New Yorker*:

Heller uses nonsense, satire, non sequiturs, slapstick, and farce. He wallows in his own laughter and finally drowns in it. What remains is a debris of sour jokes, stage anger, dirty words, synthetic looniness, and the sort of antic behavior the children fall into when they know they are losing our attention.[3]

If this kind of criticism is too negligent and easy, presuming to register the author's state of mind as he produces his work, a more serious criticism of the novel and one which suggests several points for consideration is made by R. G. Stern in *The New York Times Book Review*:

Catch-22 has much passion, comic and fervent, but it gasps for want of craft and sensibility. . . . Joseph Heller is like a brilliant painter who decides to throw all the ideas in his sketchbooks onto one canvas, relying on their charm and shock to compensate for the lack of design. . . . The

---

[1] Nelson Algren, "The Catch," *Nation*, 193 (November 4, 1961), 358.

[2] Julian Mitchell, "Under Mad Gods," *Spectator* (London), 208 (June 15, 1962), 801.

[3] Whitney Balliett, *New Yorker*, 37 (December 9, 1961), 247.

book is an emotional hodge-podge; no mood is sustained long enough
to register for more than a chapter.[4]

While this indictment is overstated, especially the last statement,
and while it misses certain unifying elements in the novel, it does
point to strengths and weaknesses in the book. Even the book's most
fervid admirers are forced to admit that a judicious pruning might
have helped; and all but the most superficial of the book's detractors
admit at least flashes of comic brilliance in the author's style.

The title, *Catch-22*, refers to that rider which seems to be attached
to every code of the rights of men and which gives those in authority
the power to revoke those rights at will. It has many clauses in the
novel, the most memorable being that recorded in a conversation
between Yossarian and the squadron medical officer, Doc Daneeka,
concerning Yossarian's tent-mate Orr, who they both agree is crazy
and should be grounded.

All he had to do was ask; and as soon as he did, he would no longer be
crazy and would have to fly more missions. Orr would be crazy to fly
more missions and sane if he didn't, but if he was sane he had to fly
them. If he flew them he was crazy and didn't have to; but if he didn't
want to he was sane and had to. Yossarian was moved very deeply by
the absolute simplicity of this clause of Catch-22 and let out a respectful
whistle.

"That's some catch, that Catch-22," he observed.
"It's the best there is," Doc Daneeka agreed.[5]

For Yossarian it is a closed system leading only to his death, and
every seeming exit is blocked as he makes for it. Since the colonel
seems prepared to raise the required number of bombing missions
indefinitely, he doesn't see any escape from annihilation. He goes to
the mail clerk who seems to be running everything, ex-P. F. C.
Wintergreen.

[4] R. G. Stern, *New York Times Book Review* (October 22, 1961), p. 50.

[5] Joseph Heller, *Catch-22* (New York: Simon & Schuster, 1961; repr. New York: Dell, 1962). Further references are to the latter edition.

"What would they do to me," he asked in confidential tones, "if I refused to fly them?"

"We'd probably shoot you," ex-P.F.C. Wintergreen replied.

"*We?*" Yossarian cried in surprise. "What do you mean, *we?* Since when are you on their side?"

"If you're going to be shot, whose side do you expect me to be on?" (p. 60)

Courage, loyalty, all the standard wartime virtues give way to the need to survive in the face of imminent annihilation.

The answer of Dunbar, Yossarian's friend, to the imminence of death is to cultivate boredom by doing such things as striking up conversations with patriotic Texans. The years are slipping away from him, he tells Clevinger, whose idealism rings hollow in this atmosphere, and he is being carried too quickly toward his death. He is an old man already, because on every mission he is only inches away from death.

"Well, maybe it's true," Clevinger conceded unwillingly in a subdued tone. "Maybe a long life does have to be filled with many irrational conditions if it's to seem long. But in that event, who wants one?"

"I do," Dunbar told him.

"Why?" Clevinger asked.

"What else is there?" (p. 40)

Part of the dilemma is here. Life may be seen as irrational and even absurd, but beyond it looms an almost palpable nothingness, a void beyond life which is as much the experience of modern man, as expressed by Hemingway's *nada*, as is the unreason within life: "What did he fear? It was not fear or dread. It was a nothing that he knew too well. It was all a nothing and man was nothing too. . . . Some lived in it and never felt it but he knew it all was nada y pues nada y nada y pues nada."[6] Certainly this nothing is very real to

[6] Ernest Hemingway, "A Clean, Well-Lighted Place," *The Snows of Kilimanjaro and Other Stories* (New York: Charles Scribner's Sons, 1927; repr. New York: Charles Scribner's Sons, 1961), p. 32.

Yossarian. In the beginning of the novel other people exist for him primarily as they threaten his existence, are necessary to his survival, or as he puzzles over their estrangement from themselves in their absorption with principles which in the face of nothingness are simply without meaning.

The question of madness and sanity is central to the book's technique. The apparent sanity of some of the characters and the apparent insanity of others is revealed time and again as only apparent. Our first remembrance of *Catch-22* is probably of the many vivid characters throughout the novel. Many of the most vivid of these seem grotesques and madmen. Dunbar, for example, seeks out and cultivates boredom to "make the time go slow." Orr as a boy walked around with crab apples in his cheeks, or, as he says, " 'When I couldn't get crab apples . . . I used horse chestnuts. Horse chestnuts are about the same size as crab apples and actually have a better shape, although the shape doesn't matter a bit' " (p. 23). And the maddest of all the book's characters seems to be the hero, Captain John Yossarian.

Yossarian first appears malingering in a hospital, moodily censoring all the modifiers in the letters of enlisted men and signing the censor's name "Washington Irving," or, for variety, "Irving Washington." Crazy, it seems; but this madness of his begins to assume a different aspect when set beside the activities of the same people around him. Clevinger, for example, knows that Yossarian is crazy and tells him so.

> "They're trying to kill me," Yossarian told him calmly.
> "No one's trying to kill you," Clevinger cried.
> "Then why are they shooting at me?" Yossarian asked.
> "They're shooting at *everyone*," Clevinger answered. "They're trying to kill everyone."
> "And what difference does that make?"
> Clevinger was already on the way, half out of his chair with emotion, his eyes moist and his lips quivering and pale. As always occurred when he quarreled over principles in which he believed passionately, he would

end up gasping furiously and blinking back bitter tears of conviction. There were many principles in which Clevinger believed passionately. He was crazy. (p. 17)

The satire entwined in the farce, the painful twinge in even the most humorous parts of the book, is revealed in such a passage. In such a situation the examination of traditionally assumed values becomes literally a matter of life or death. Yossarian least of all could be content to be just a portion of a faceless *everyone*, to die or not as chance wills. He is, the book says elsewhere, willing to be the victim of anything but circumstance.

In the face of the threats to his existence Yossarian has only one overriding principle—to stay alive—and to that end he malingers in a hospital, sabotages his plane, puts soap in the squadron's food, alters a combat map, and even at one time toys with the idea of murdering his commanding officer. He is, in short, the kind of character that the term "*anti*hero" should have been reserved for. Many who are given this title are simply "*non*heros"—weak, ineffectual little men, little more than anguished consciousnesses. Yossarian, however, is aggressively, even belligerently, antiheroic, and in his antiheroism is a direct challenge to the values and ideals which the world claims to hold.

This challenge to these values and ideals is given telling expression in an exchange between Nately—like Clevinger a young man of high ideals—and a cynical old Italian. Nately is the kind of romantic figure who might have been the hero of the novel if it had been of the more traditional type of war novels. Like Prewitt in *From Here to Eternity*, for example, he is totally committed to his ideals; like Prewitt he is in love with a prostitute; and like Prewitt he is accidentally killed. But he is far from being the hero of this novel. The hero of this novel is Yossarian, and although Yossarian may be in constant danger of becoming a victim, he will never be a *pathetic* victim. The cynical old Italian indicates in an exchange with Nately just what is wrong with the younger man's outlook.

"They are going to kill you if you don't watch out, and I can see now that you are not going to watch out. Why don't you use some sense and try to be more like me? You might live to be a hundred and seven, too."

"Because it's better to die on one's feet than live on one's knees," Nately retorted with triumphant and lofty conviction. "I guess you've heard that saying before."

"Yes, I certainly have," mused the treacherous old man, smiling again. "But I'm afraid you have it backward. It is better to *live* on one's feet than die on one's knees. *That* is the way the saying goes." (pp. 253–254)

There is a lucidity in this which reveals in the lofty pretensions of the sane and principled young men in the novel who are so un-aware of the threat to their existence the very depth of absurdity. Indeed, integral to *Catch-22* is the notion of the absurd. This is true not only of the thematic implications of the novel but is central to its technique. A partial definition of the absurd by Camus is relevant to one aspect of the theme of the novel: "This discomfort in the face of man's own inhumanity, this incalculable tumble before the image of what we are, this 'nausea,' as a writer of today calls it, is also the absurd."[7]

Both in content and technique, *Catch-22* has affinities with the theatre of the absurd. We may see the affinity of the novel to the technique of absurd drama in the following description by Martin Esslin: "The means by which the dramatists of the Absurd express their critique . . . of our disintegrating society are based on sud-denly confronting their audiences with a grotesquely heightened and distorted picture of a world that has gone mad."[8] Esslin adds,

As the incomprehensibility of the motives and the often unexplained and mysterious nature of the Characters' actions in the Theatre of the

[7] Albert Camus, *The Myth of Sisyphus and Other Essays*, trans. Justin O'Brien (New York: Vintage Books, 1955), p. 11.
[8] Martin Esslin, *The Theatre of the Absurd* (New York: Anchor Books, 1961), p. 300.

Absurd effectively prevent identification, such theatre is a comic theatre in spite of the fact that its subject matter is somber, violent and bitter. That is why the Theatre of the Absurd transcends the categories of comedy and tragedy and combines laughter with horror.[9]

This combination of laughter with horror occurs throughout *Catch-22* and has caused it to be placed with other works in recent fiction called "black humor."

The technique of "black humor" seems to have evolved in response to the needs of an age whose sensibilities have been largely blunted. As a technique, the humor serves to lower the reader's defenses so that the full force of the horror may be felt. One flaw in the usual novel out of World War II is that the piling up of horror upon horror finally makes the reader immune. In an age which has made a daily companion of horror (so that indifference has become a mode of survival), some change of technique is needed from the naturalistic accumulation of detail, which is designed to tell on the reader by its sheer weight and which is characteristic of most recent war novels; some new way is required to reach the reader once again and involve him.

Despite the presence of other novels in the list of works called "black humor," the term has not been explored well enough to shed much light on any particular work placed on the list. The detractors of *Catch-22* have usually regarded it as a disorderly mixture of comedy, satire, farce, and invective; the book's admirers, on the other hand, have stressed the basic seriousness and purpose beneath the apparently disorganized and purposeless surface. Julian Mitchell, an admirer, called it "a surrealist Iliad, with a lunatic High Command instead of gods, and a coward for a hero" and went on to label it "one of the finest examples of the genre in which many of the best modern novels are written, that of the anguished farce (or, literally, the horror-comic)."[10] This is perceptive, and it indicates

---

[9] *Ibid.*, p. 301.
[10] Mitchell, "Under Mad Gods," p. 801.

what is lacking in a reading of the humor as simply jokes which go sour. The *Catch-22* joke is not even very funny the first time, and in fact, as we soon learn, it is no joke.

In the longest and in many ways the most perceptive review of the novel, Robert Brustein called the novel "a picaresque epic," and, however unfamiliar such a combination may seem, we may begin a description of the book by holding to these two descriptions of it as an "anguished farce" and a "picaresque epic." The first term will account for the reaction to the book on the one hand as slapstick and on the other as intensely serious, while the second term— "picaresque epic"—can help to make clearer a structure which is *not* formless but which is also not in the Jamesian "well-made novel" tradition.

Perhaps it was Evelyn Waugh who began the development of what Mitchell calls the "anguished farce." In *Vile Bodies* the final image of the General and a prostitute named Chastity engaged in sex in a staff car while the sounds of battle commence around them has in it this combination of comedy and horror. So have the novels of Nathanael West. Certainly the two trials in *Catch-22* recall both Kafka and West.

> "Everything's going to be all right, Chaplain," the major said encouragingly. "You've got nothing to be afraid of if you're not guilty. What are you so afraid of? You're not guilty, are you?"
>
> "Sure he's guilty," said the colonel. "Guilty as hell."
>
> "Guilty of what?" implored the chaplain, feeling more and more bewildered and not knowing which of the men to appeal to for mercy. The third officer wore no insignia and lurked in silence off to the side. "What did I do?"
>
> "That's just what we're going to find out," answered the colonel . . . (p. 389)

The specific tradition of the absurd not only operates on the social level, pillorying the cruel idiocies of society, as in Waugh's early novels, but, as Esslin says, faces up to a deeper layer of absurdity—the absurdity of the human condition itself in a world where the decline of religious belief has deprived man of certainties. When it is no longer possible to accept simple and complete systems of values and revelations of divine purpose, life must be faced in its ultimate stark reality.[11]

As *Catch-22* begins, Yossarian has already faced the stark reality of his approaching death and nothingness, though at this point the reader is aware only of the result—a man almost beside himself at the thought of death. The event which has brought him the message of his own mortality is the death of Snowden, a gunner in Yossarian's plane. Yossarian spent the better part of a flight home trying to minister to the dying gunner, only to find that the wound he was treating was not the fatal one; the fatal wound—mortality itself—was not subject to first aid. Mortality returns like a theme in music, each time with variations of meaning, but each time essentially the same. When questions are asked for at a briefing session, Yossarian asks the question which is always with him:

"Where are the Snowdens of yesteryear?"

"I'm afraid I don't understand."

"Où sont les Neigedens d'antan?" Yossarian said to make it easier for him.

"Parlez en anglais, for Christ's sake," said the corporal, *"Je ne parle pas français."*

"Neither do I," answered Yossarian, who was ready to pursue him through all the words in the world to wring the knowledge from him if he could. (p. 36)

Yossarian not only lives on the edge of the void as the others do, but lives in constant knowledge of that void. The void has become "eloquent" for him as Camus says in *The Myth of Sisyphus*:

In certain situations, replying "nothing" when asked what one is thinking about may be pretense in a man. Those who are loved are well aware of this. But if that reply is sincere, if it symbolizes that odd state of soul

[11] Esslin, *The Theatre of the Absurd*, p. 292.

in which the void becomes eloquent, in which the chain of daily gestures is broken, in which the heart vainly seeks the link that will con-
nect it again, then it is as it were the first sign of absurdity.[12]

Once the thing has been done it seems inevitable: where else to
find the very quintessence of the absurd other than in a modern
military establishment in the middle of a modern war? This is
what every ex-military man misses in so many novels to come out
of World War II and the Korean War—that sense of grotesqueness
of the situation, the irrationality and inadequacy of the means for
survival, and in general a feeling of mingled terror and unreality.
In short, the elements requisite to literature of the absurd.

In literature of the absurd the apparently ordered surface of
reality is torn away to reveal the chaos and unreason beneath. Paradox, therefore, is the very essence of the technique of literature of
the absurd. Traditional reason is revealed as unreason because it
supposes an ordered, rational world. Sanity in the traditional sense
is really insanity; that is, if sanity is the ability to come to terms
with reality, then it is insane to act as if the world is coherent and
rational. Loyalty to traditional institutions can be disloyalty to oneself simply because the institutions may threaten the people they
are ostensibly designed to serve.

Part of the difference between *Catch-22* and the usual war novel
lies in this insistent world-view of a nothingness which threatens to
invade even the selves of these men. A naturalistic novel, after all,
keeps the integrity of the self, however that self may be buffeted
about and even destroyed. In the world of *Catch-22*, however, the
void is not only a constant presence; it also threatens to invade the
self and it has its ally in a system which would make of these men
anonymous and expendable cogs in a war machine so devoted to
the purposes of men like Colonel Cathcart and General Peckem as
to make the objective of winning the war almost an afterthought.

Throughout the book men are "disappeared," a chillingly apt

[12] Camus, *The Myth of Sisyphus*, p. 10.

term. Dunbar, Clevinger, Major Major—in one way or another all seem to die or disappear. The terms of life or death, existence or nonexistence are irrational and arbitrary. Mudd, a man who was to have lived in Yossarian's tent but who was killed before he reported for duty, is alive administratively because to admit his death would be sloppy bookkeeping. Doc Daneeka, on the other hand, is administratively dead and spends the rest of his time forlornly trying to assert his existence. The faceless anonymity of the system is expressed in the career of this little man, throughout much of the book an eager accomplice of the system and one who has called the war a "godsend," only to spend the rest of his time trying to get those still within the system to recognize his existence. He finally loses his last link with a world in which he can exist when his wife moves, leaving no forwarding address after receiving a form letter of condolence: "Dear Mrs., Mr., Miss, or Mr. and Mrs. Daneeka: Words cannot express the deep personal grief I experienced when your husband, son, father or brother was killed, wounded or reported missing in action" (p. 354).

The ultimate in faceless inhumanity is achieved in the figure of the soldier in white:

> The soldier in white was constructed entirely of gauze, plaster and a thermometer, and the thermometer was merely an adornment left balanced in the empty dark hole in the bandages over his mouth early each morning and late each afternoon by Nurse Cramer and Nurse Duckett right up to the afternoon Nurse Cramer read the thermometer and discovered he was dead. (p. 171)

The other patients take offense against him, "rebelling against his presence as a ghastly imposition and resenting him malevolently for the nauseating truth of which he was a bright reminder" (p. 172). The soldier in white is not only a reminder of the imminence of death; he is also a constant reminder to the men of their status within the system. The nurses have two jars, one to drip liquid into the soldier in white and the other to catch the liquid. At the end of the process, the two jars are reversed. " 'Why can't they hook the two jars up to each other and eliminate the middleman?' the artillery captain with whom Yossarian had stopped playing chess inquired. 'What the hell do they need him for?' " (p. 174). The reappearance of the soldier in white later is too much for Dunbar, who goes berserk.

"It's the same one!" Dunbar shouted at him emphatically in a voice rising clearly above the raucous commotion. "Don't you understand? It's the same one."

"The same one!" Yossarian heard himself echo, quivering with a deep and ominous excitement that he could not control, and shoved his way after Dunbar toward the bed of the soldier in white. . . .

It was indeed the same man. He had lost a few inches and added some weight, but Yossarian remembered him instantly by the two stiff arms and the two stiff, thick, useless legs drawn upward into the air almost perpendicularly by the taut ropes and the long lead weights suspended from pulleys over him and by the frayed black hole in the bandages over his mouth. . . .

"There's no one inside!" Dunbar yelled at him unexpectedly. (p. 374)

Whether because Dunbar has guessed some secret of the system or because he is simply inconvenient, he is immediately "disappeared." Throughout the book, humor is mingled with a horror that at times, as in this image of men being "disappeared," is reminiscent of *1984*.

Such then is the atmosphere of *Catch-22*. There is a danger that in thus insisting on the seriousness underlying the humor, the humor of the book may be slighted. Almost no one, however, is prepared to deny the existence of this humor and even to accept it, at least at times, as being of a very high quality. The greater danger is to fall into the trap of too easily dismissing the novel as a hodge-podge of comic scenes by a novelist who is unable to maintain the comedy. The comic is an integral element in the novel, as it is in much literature of the absurd, but, also like other absurd literature, it is present in a merging of the often ridiculous with the always desperate.

The larger structure of the novel is episodic, with a succession of scenes following and sometimes interrupting each other like a jumbled series of playlets. At first glance these successive scenes seem related only in that they take place somewhere within the purview of the hero, John Yossarian. Gradually, however, they reveal the same pervasive atmosphere of fear, anxiety, and what Sartre has called the nausea of existence, all in something like an asylum for the criminally insane. As this atmosphere begins to become apparent the movement of the book becomes clearer. These apparently only tangentially related scenes have their relevance to the spiritual development of the book's hero.

At the beginning Yossarian has become fully aware of himself by becoming aware of the threat to himself; this awareness causes him to struggle violently to detach himself in order to survive. The moment of his beginning the attempt to detach himself has been the moment of his experience of Snowden's death; and his initial expression of it is to refuse to wear his uniform, the symbol of his involvement in a system which threatens to destroy him. The next response is to flee into the hospital. There is death in the hospital also, but at least in the hospital are those who can be called on for help, not because they are humane but because that is their function in the system; and death in the hospital is at least clean.

. . . outside the hospital the war was still going on. Men went mad and were rewarded with medals. All over the world, boys on every side of the bomb line were laying down their lives for what they had been told was their country, and no one seemed to mind, least of all the boys who were laying down their young lives. There was no end in sight. (p. 16)

Awareness of self such as Yossarian's is dangerous to the system and makes him hated and feared by those who serve the system with most enthusiasm. The ideal warrior now is not a heroic individual in the ancient mold, but someone unaware and consequently not quite human. Havermeyer, for example, according to Colonel

Cathcart, is "the best damned bombardier we've got" (p. 30). He seems absolutely unaware of the threat of death (until his sudden awareness near the end of the book); he is also a man who spends his evenings shooting field mice with dumdummed bullets.

Not only are many of the victims of the system unaware, the system itself seems to be solely in the hands of those who exist as little more than creatures of their need to succeed within the terms of the system. When Lieutenant Colonel Korn offers his immoral deal to Yossarian, he tells him,

> "And there you have the crux of the situation. Colonel Cathcart wants to be a general and I want to be a colonel, and that's why we have to send you home."
> "Why does he want to be a general?"
> "Why? For the same reason that I want to be a colonel. What else have we got to do? Everyone teaches us to aspire to higher things. A general is higher than a colonel, and a colonel is higher than a lieutenant colonel. So we're aspiring." (p. 435)

One version and perversion of the American dream is thus presented starkly. Aspiration within the system with no examination of ends has become an end in itself; it has become a substitute for meaningful life. Colonel Cathcart and Colonel Korn exist only in their attempts to use an irrational system for their own irrational ends. It is no accident that the most irrational of them all, Scheisskopf, finally is put in charge. Modern evil exists in these men not in any overpowering, demonic guise, but in the guise of Horatio Alger dutifully climbing to success over the bleeding forms of his fellows.

Dutiful obedience is presented throughout the book as the height of madness. Clevinger is not merely a dutiful but a passionate supporter of the system. And he is a dope. Appleby is an all-American boy who wins at all games like Tom Stover at Yale and who dutifully reports Yossarian's attempt to malinger by catching malaria. He is only presented as sane when he comes to Yossarian after the latter has refused to fly any more and tells him, "I hope you do get away with it" (p. 409).

Perhaps the most frightening character of all is Aarfy, who is so committed to clichés that he seems to have no substance at all. In his playful moods Aarfy likes to come into the nose of the plane and jab Yossarian as he wildly directs the pilot away from flak.

"I said get *out of here!*" Yossarian shouted and broke into tears. He began punching Aarfy in the body with both hands as hard as he could. "Get *away* from me! *Get away!*"

Punching Aarfy was like sinking his fists into a limp sack of inflated rubber. There was no resistance, no response at all from the soft, insensitive mass. . . .

Yossarian was dumbfounded by his state of rapturous contentment. Aarfy was like an eerie ogre in a dream, incapable of being bruised or evaded, and Yossarian dreaded him for a complex of reasons he was too petrified to untangle. (pp. 153–154)

Aarfy is a climber who works on Nately because Nately's father is rich and may give him a job; he divides all women into good ones and bad ones, and dates only the ones whose fathers can help him; he is prepared at the end to give perjured testimony against Yossarian at the request of Colonel Cathcart. In short, he is not only devoted to the same kind of success as the Cathcarts and Peckems, but his commitment is so complete as to make him inhuman.

Paradoxically (in terms of an older literary tradition) disengagement in this novel is not immoral but moral. The literature of social criticism of the thirties, for example, insisted that one finds himself only in social involvement. In *Catch-22* such involvement is the way to lose oneself, as the case of Appleby and others shows. It is as Yossarian disengages himself that he finds himself.

This is apparently what Brustein means when he calls the book a "picaresque epic." Yossarian is a picaro in that he is at odds with the role which society would thrust upon him, but by the end of the novel he is more than just a picaro, at least by intention. He has become what R. W. B. Lewis calls a "picaresque saint": ". . . in what seems to me the most fully developed portraits of the contemporary hero, he is apt to share not only the miseries of humanity, but its gravest weaknesses, too, and even in its sins. He is not only a saint, as the novelists have been describing him. He is a picaresque saint."[13]

The structure of *Catch-22*, broadly, derives from Yossarian's struggle to detach himself in order to survive to a realization, convincing or not, that his detaching himself has a larger meaning. The process of disengaging himself from the institutions which threaten to victimize him leads to his total moral engagement with others. He accepts his guilt (as Camus says that each man must) in the form of being the target of Nately's whore, and he refuses the sure but immoral survival offered by Korn and Cathcart in favor of a much less certain but at least morally acceptable survival on his own terms. He chooses, as the old man says, to live on his feet rather than to die—or live—on his knees. The episodes concerning Orr have foreshadowed this change; the persuasiveness of the change is another question.

The disjunctive, episodic nature of the novel's structure is a real challenge to the artist's ability to make an organic whole, and Heller does not always succeed, particularly in the episodes involving Milo Minderbinder, the budding tycoon. That Heller is able on the whole to succeed in making these elements a unified whole, that he is able even to hold the reader through an initially bewildering series of wild scenes is due in no small part to his gift for constructing vital, memorable characters. Chief White Halfoat, who is determined to die of pneumonia, Hungry Joe, who is at peace only in combat and who finally dies in his sleep, suffocated by the same cat with which he had his most memorable battles, Major ———— de Coverley, ex-P.F.C. Wintergreen—the book overflows with characters who come to life in a sentence or two. Part of the meaning of the book, in fact, is in their enduring individuality in the grip of a system which threatens that individuality and their very existence.

The abrupt shifts in time and event are also not flaws of the book;

[13] R. W. B. Lewis, *The Picaresque Saint* (New York: J. B. Lippincott, 1958), p. 32.

rather they are central to its technique. These are not really flash-backs, because they are not related either to a character's specific remembrance nor are they often explicitly related to the situation which they interrupt. One of the functions of these abrupt time-shifts, like Heller's use of paradox, is, to wrench the characters out of the traditionally ordered, time-bound context of the novel. Events exist primarily not in any cause-and-effect or chronological relation to one another but simultaneously. This does not mean that time has been escaped in the novel; on the contrary, it has become more personal and hence more crucial. Because of the nearness of the book's characters to death, time is literally running out on them. Clock time is related to the notion of a measured, ordered eternity. For Yossarian, however, there is no God and therefore no eternity; there is only the space until his death and everything conspires to shorten this space.

This suggests why the last part of the novel is unconvincing. Despite the fact that the episodes of Orr are designed to foreshadow the change which takes place in Yossarian in the last part, the change is less than convincing. Like Yossarian, Orr seems to be crazy, but unlike Yossarian he has method in his madness. Orr is Yossarian's tentmate, who keeps telling two apparently pointless stories. One story is about his practice as a boy of keeping crab apples or, when he couldn't get crab apples, horse chestnuts in his cheeks. The other story is a reminder to Yossarian of the time when Orr stood laughing while an Italian prostitute hit him over the head with her shoe. As the two apparently most insane men in the outfit, the men have a fellow feeling which causes Yossarian to feel that Orr is trying to tell him something.

. . . Yossarian was willing to give Orr the benefit of the doubt because Orr was from the wilderness outside New York City and knew so much more about wild-life than Yossarian did, and because Orr, unlike Yossarian's mother, father, sister, brother, aunt, uncle, in-law, teacher, spiritual leader, legislator, neighbor and newspaper, had never lied to him about anything crucial. (p. 47)

When he hears that Orr has made it to Sweden, Yossarian understands what Orr has been trying to tell him. The crab apples were to
give him a look of apple-cheeked innocence, which is the only defense in a world where everything and everyone threatens. But the
speeches of the characters are clues to the unnatural quality of the
style of the last part of the book. The chaplain exclaims, " 'It's a
miracle of human perseverance, I tell you. And that's just what I'm
going to do from now on! I'm going to persevere. Yes, I'm going to
persevere' " (p. 459). Even Yossarian's speech is changed: " 'Oh,
why didn't I listen to him? Why wouldn't I have some faith?' " (p.
459).

Both the event of Orr's escape to Sweden and the meaning of it,
then, have been amply foreshadowed throughout much of the novel.
But the meaning of Orr's escape doesn't seem to fit with Yossarian's
decision in the last of the book. When the chaplain asks Yossarian
why the girl was hitting Orr with her shoe, he answers, " 'Because
he was paying her to, that's why! But she wouldn't hit him hard
enough, so he had to row to Sweden' " (p. 460). The message seems
straightforward enough: in a world where he is constantly threat-
ened with annihilation, a man must use enormous cleverness and
resourcefulness to survive. This seems in keeping with Yossarian's
growing feeling from the beginning; Orr's message is simply that
survival is indeed possible. But somehow Yossarian's final decision is
supposed to go beyond this doctrine of survival to a doctrine of social
involvement. The last four or five chapters are devoted to this
change, and indicative of the difficulty which the author apparently
had in making this change convincing. Both atmosphere and technique change.

The book has two major flaws. In the first place, some of the material does not fit in. The picaresque structure allows a great deal of
latitude, but the *atmosphere* must be consistent. In the midst of matters as momentous as life and death, such episodes as that of the
Great Loyalty Oath Crusade seem excrescences. This is a voice from
the postwar as is the inordinate space given to the enterprises of

Milo Minderbinder, including his strafing of his own men on com-
mission from the enemy. The second flaw is greater. In keeping with
the nature of the picaresque novel as standing outside society and
making mostly negative comments upon it, the picaresque novelist
often has difficulty in ending his novel, especially on a positive note.
The last four chapters of the novel have a discursive quality not
found in most of the other parts of the novel. The long philosophical
argument between Yossarian and the ex-college professor is out of
keeping with the technique of the rest of the book, in which actions
and situations speak for themselves. In short, the book loses its dramatic quality.

This loss of the dramatic quality at the end of the novel points to
an even deeper problem, the change in Yossarian. The first part of
his story, his reaction to death and his need to disengage himself
from all that threatens him, is made poignantly convincing; the last
stage of his development, the decision that there is something greater
than survival, is not so convincing. Yossarian's morality in saying
'no' to the forces which threaten to take him over is supposed to become a morality of social involvement; he is to go to Sweden to try
to do something about all of the horrors he has seen in his last night
in Rome.

It is possible to intellectualize this result: if Yossarian were to accept the deal offered him in order to survive, he might still lose his
self to the system. We might even accept the point that Yossarian's
whole career has been pointing toward this moment of total rebellion, of total refusal—the act of complete disengagement which is
desertion. The flaw is that the end is not artistically convincing. In
his all-absorbing involvement in the threat to his own existence, Yossarian has been so little aware of the threat to others that the sudden
change to an awareness of them and dedication to trying to help
them does not have the same force.

This is a familiar difficulty for several of the strains of literature
represented in *Catch-22*. The comic writer whose comedy has been
critical and biting often has the difficulty of restoring order to a con-

text which has been thoroughly disordered for comic effect. The absurdist writer has constant difficulty, having shown the logic of alienation and estrangement from life, in trying to restore a meaningful link to that life. The picaro who so determinedly disengages himself from society and the human institutions which strive to restrict him can only with difficulty become engaged again with his kind without at the same time becoming engaged with the institutions of his kind.

This difficulty of the ending of *Catch-22* is not fatal to the success of the novel; far from it. At the present time there is little literature of the absurd, black humor, or any other classification into which this novel might seem to fall which supplies a convincing, viable solution to the essentially negative treatment which it gives to modern life. The convincing positive elements in the novel are connected with the first three quarters, in which characters live and live vitally in the teeth of almost insuperable odds for death and anonymity. The discursive elements near the end, while eloquent, miss the success of the earlier dramatic portions because they belie an implicit theme of the novel: that which argues about and abstracts from each character betrays what is uniquely his own—his individuality— and is allied to the threat of facelessness and annihilation which he must constantly confront and oppose. In traditional literature, the ideal is juxtaposed to the real in order to demonstrate the falling away of the real from the ideal. In the paradox of absurd literature, the real and the ideal are radically incompatible; hence the ideal is largely irrelevant and even destructive. Yossarian's strength is not only that he consciously and resolutely *is*, but that he constantly rejects attempts to make him over in terms of any ideal. He is a compelling creation and probably the shape of many heroes to come. As a man in the novel says of him,

"That crazy bastard may be the only sane one left!" (p. 114)

George and Martha: Sad, Sad, Sad

Anthony Channell Hilfer

Edward Albee's play *Who's Afraid of Virginia Woolf* opened on October 13, 1962, at the Billy Rose Theater in New York City. Although this was Albee's first Broadway play, he was no stranger to the theatre-going public, having become well known through his off-Broadway short dramas, *The American Dream* and *The Zoo Story*. The challenge he faced was to show that he could produce a full-length drama of equal intensity to that of his short plays and entertain with it a less specialized audience than frequents off-Broadway dramas.

Most critics felt he proved his ability to write a well-constructed full-length play, and the play's run demonstrated its considerable popularity with audiences. But the enthusiastic reception of the play was not unmixed by controversy and dissent. Some objected to the trickiness of the dramatic devices Albee employed while others saw the play as obscene and decadent.

The reason for the accusation of obscenity can be found by considering the following summary compiled by Alfred Chester:

Virginia Woolf gives us four almost unrelievably nasty people who for something like three-and-a-half hours, our time and theirs, take part in a drunken orgy of backbiting, bitchery, humiliation, verbal castration, exposure, and physical mauling. Among them are the following weaknesses, crimes, and sins, imputed or established, sometimes duplicated or even quadruplicated: deceit, treachery, impotence, alcoholism, abortion, incest, patricide, matricide, attempted uxoricide, phantom filicide, and others more trivial like adultery and pederasty . . .[1]

I ought to mention that little of this takes place on stage; it is mostly talked about.

[1] Alfred Chester, "Edward Albee: Red Herrings and White Whales," *Commentary*, XXXV (April, 1963), 297.

The play was also called "decadent." One critic, in an article brilliantly entitled, "Who's Afraid of Edward Albee?," claims that Albee's play "gratifies an adolescent culture which likes to think of itself as decadent."[2] The critic indignantly refutes Albee's belief that America is decadent, although he fails to explain how we can distinguish people who like to think they are decadent from people who *really are* decadent.

Decadence is indeed a theme in the play, though perhaps less major than the aforementioned critic would have us believe. Albee does name his college town "New Carthage" and at one point in the play we find George portentously reading aloud a passage from *The Decline of the West*. The decadence theme extends to characterization as well. One major sign of decadence has always been the switching of sexual roles. Thus Juvenal in his satires shows the decadence of Rome in his diatribes upon men who wear make-up and behave in a generally putrescent fashion and women who dress in gladiator's clothing and sweatily fight with each other. And, to pick a more recent example, a Southern lady novelist, Augusta Jane Evans, predicted during Reconstruction the imminent downfall of the decadent North. Her evidence that retribution was on hand was that during a visit to New York she saw effeminate men and masculine women.[3] Without any imputation of error to Augusta Jane Evans's powers of observation, it seems fair to note that the decline and fall she predicted have been at the very least somewhat delayed.

Perhaps Albee is similarly in error, for he also depicts decadence in terms of the reversal of roles. In our introduction to the characters we find Martha, the woman, cursing vigorously and George, the man, prissily objecting. Martha is direct and violent. George, on the other hand, is nothing if not "catty." He responds to an argu-

---

[2] Richard Schechner, "Who's Afraid of Edward Albee?," *Tulane Drama Review*, VII, No. 3 (Spring, 1963), 7–10.

[3] Ben W. Griffith, Jr., ed., "A Lady Novelist Views the Reconstruction: An Augusta Jane Evans Letter," *Georgia Historical Quarterly*, XLIII, No. 3 (March, 1959), 103–104.

ment over a movie Martha is trying to remember with "Well, that was probably before my *time*," thus reminding Martha of her age in an archetypically feminine manner. At one point, Martha appropriately calls George an "old floozy," thus confusing the literal-minded Honey who tries to work out the genders more scientifically: "He's not a floozie . . . He can't be a floozie . . . you're a floozie." One of the more harrowing moments in the drama is Martha's description of how she once accidentally knocked George cold in an impromptu boxing match. She believes, plausibly enough, that this colored their whole life.

In the boxing match as elsewhere Martha plays a dominant, masculine, sadistic role, whereas George is subordinate, passive, masochistic. Now as William Stekel, the author of the well-known treatise *Sadism and Masochism*, has pointed out, the behavior of sado-masochists exhibits a strong element of the childish. The sickness of the sado-masochist is essentially a regression to childishness. Albee's characters, perfectly fitting this pattern, are all children and very naughty ones at that. Martha, for instance, calls out appallingly to George: "C'mon over here and give your mommy a big sloppy kiss." Shortly later, Martha baby-talks: "I'm firsty." But the most obvious examples of childishness are not in the baby talk but in the games the characters play. "Fun and Games" is the title of the first act but the fun and games continue throughout the drama. Martha's knockout victory was a game, however serious the consequences; she was even wearing boxing gloves at the time. A letter to *Commentary* acutely notes how much of the action is summarized in perverse parodies of alliterative children's games: "Humiliate the Host," "Hump the Hostess," "Get the Guests."[4] If some of these games are obviously obscene, so are many children's games—playing doctor, for instance. Even the adultery between Nick and Martha is a game, played mostly for George's benefit, just as children often invent games and rituals for the purpose of

[4] Anthony and Dolores Filandro, letter to *Commentary*, XXXVI (October, 1963), 272.

excluding or humiliating other children. In the second act, in the midst of his most extreme humiliation, George screams out in fury that "THE GAME IS OVER!" But when Martha and Nick insist on finishing their game of "Humiliate the Host," George invokes the child's rule of fairness for his game of "Get the Guests": "This is my game! You played yours . . . you people. This is my game!" George gets another small revenge when Nick loses one of Martha's games and becomes a "houseboy." In a parodied cliché, George sums up the situation: "Vicious children, with their oh-so-sad games, hopscotching their way through life, etcetera, etcetera."

The essential game throughout is the war game between George and Martha; the other games are simply variations of this. Nick and Honey are immediately involved in the war game as George wins a small tactical victory by opening the door to the unsuspecting guests at the very moment when Martha is roaring out an obscenity. Nick and Honey become pawns in the combat between George and Martha, and Martha's flirtation and subsequent adultery with Nick proceed more from tactics than from lust. Albee brilliantly develops his drama of psychological warfare but the notion is not new. Strindberg's *The Dance of Death* is built around a similar war between men and women. In Strindberg's play, as in Albee's, an outsider becomes a pawn in the bitter conflict, and in both plays is the suggestion that the relationship between the two combatants is a mixture of hate and love and that this complicated and perverse relationship is both the prison and the necessary opiate of the characters. As the pawn in the conflict remarks, "That's known as *love-hatred* and comes from the lowest depths."[5]

More of an influence on Albee than Strindberg's play was Eugene O'Neill's *Long Day's Journey into Night*. Both *Virginia Woolf* and *Long Day's Journey* are "emotionally shattering," as the *Newsweek* review very accurately commented. In an interview with Melwyn Gussow of *Newsweek*, however, Albee complained about

[5] August Strindberg, "The Dance of Death," *Twelve Plays*, trans. Elizabeth Sprigge (London: Constable, 1963), p. 365.

comparison between his play and O'Neill's: "If you mean that both 'Long Day's Journey into Night' and 'Who's Afraid of Virginia Woolf?' have four characters and they talk a great deal and nothing happens, if you mean that, that's pretty superficial."[6] But, at the same time, Albee admits that *Long Day's Journey* was a direct influence upon *Virginia Woolf* just as Tennessee Williams' *Suddenly Last Summer* influenced *The Zoo Story*.

If Strindberg influenced the content of *Virginia Woolf*, O'Neill influenced the form. The influence was largely a matter of having four characters and they talk a great deal and nothing happens, superficial though this may be. Perhaps criticism is largely a matter of having the courage of one's superficialities and I would like to pursue the formal qualities of these plays with few characters and much talk. A possible term for both plays might be the "drama of erosion." I adopt this term, which is provisional and admittedly awkward, on the analogy of W. M. Frohock's description of the "novel of erosion" in *The Novel of Violence in America*. Mr. Frohock compares the "novel of violence," in which a character or situation is revealed through some sudden act of violence, to the "novel of erosion," in which various characters are shown as the victims of the corrosive power of time. Marcel Proust's *The Remembrance of Things Past* would be a perfect example of the novel of erosion; time is the almost visible antagonist in Proust's novel and the Baron de Charlus the most evident victim of a gradual disintegration. A far lesser though much underrated American example of this genre is James T. Farrell's novel *Studs Lonigan*, about a character who is destroyed because of not knowing what to make of time.

It is just here that a confusion would seem to enter in. Albee's play covers only a few hours in the characters' lives; although the characters are pretty well worn down by the end of the play this erosion occurred without a long-drawn process in time. Moreover,

---

[6] Melwyn Gussow, in *Newsweek*, LX, No. 18 (October 29, 1962), 52–53.

much violence is present in both *Long Day's Journey* and *Virginia Woolf*—on a verbal level at least. Thus Honey happily gurgles "Violence! Violence!" as Martha pursues one of her war games. It is violence indeed but it is important to remember that the violence is continual and uninterrupted; in neither play does a climactic point of violence lead to a new revelation of the characters and a peripety in the action. Rather both plays work by a continual pounding process, an operation analogous to the unremitting violence of a steam drill. No one act of violence is more extreme than any other. *Virginia Woolf* maintains a consistent pitch of hysteria from the start almost to the finish, while *Long Day's Journey* varies between scenes of violent recrimination and of melancholy regret. Thus, both *Virginia Woolf* and *Long Day's Journey* are filled with violence but their real affinity in form is with the novel of erosion. The wearing effect of the passage of time cannot be conveyed in the drama as in the novel, and those plays in which we see a character first as young, later as middle-aged, finally as old are more triumphs of make-up than of artistry. But the drama can gain something of the same effect by using sheer sustained pile-driving, repetition of verbal violence. Hence it should be evident that it is by the very circumscription of characters and limitation of time that *Virginia Woolf* and *Long Day's Journey* can carry out the process of wearing down the characters and spectators. The very length of the plays acts as a formal element almost numbing the audience into a punch-drunk compliance. Time actually spent at the theatre watching the same four people repeat and yet again repeat their charges and countercharges has the corrosive effect on the *spectator* of the play that the passage of time has on the *character* of the novel. Restated, my thesis is that the emotional equivalent in the drama to the long-drawn-out passage of time in a novel is the time that the spectator actually spends in the theatre. This time seems all the longer when the drama is limited to a few characters and a fixed limit of time. It is as if the spectator were really there, like Nick

and Honey, trapped at a prolonged emotional debauch. Spectators
of both plays bear out my thesis by reporting how they left O'Neill's
or Albee's play emotionally drained and exhausted. The drama
critic I quoted earlier, Alfred Chester, was impressed by the length
of Albee's play, "something like three-and-a-half hours, *our time
and theirs*" (my italics). The spectator has unforgettably lived
through the experience of the play in time. With an unskillful
playwright it is evident that an attempt at the form I have just
described would be a disaster, since obviously the audience would
leave at a certain point. I remember, in fact, that when I saw *Long
Day's Journey* the couple sitting immediately in front of me stag-
gered to their feet at the end of one act, muttered something about
needing a drink, and disappeared, never to return. To keep even
an audience with more resistance to punishment in their seats, the
playwright must sustain his repetitions without ever becoming
merely monotonous and he must allow for a certain amount of surprise without letting surprise become, more conventionally, climax.

O'Neill does this magnificently. There are surprises in the play—
Jamie's admission that his love for his brother, Edmund, was always
mixed with hatred, malice, and envy; the discovery that Mary Tyrone is on dope again—but none of these are turning points in the
play's steady, almost plodding, progression into darkness. The real
structure of the play is the repetition of emotional scenes built on
a strictly delimited set of emotions and around a few central facts.
The facts are Mary's dope addiction, Edmund's consumption, and
Jamie's stinginess. Only the consumption is a new factor in the
daily family confrontations. Both the stinginess and the addiction
are past as well as present history, compulsively remembered and
unforgiven, but such well-worn bones of contention as to call forth
routine responses of anger, shame, uneasiness, guilt, accusation, and
hopelessness. Thus, Tyrone on Jamie's worthlessness: "If you'd get
ambition in your head instead of folly! You're young yet. You could
still make your mark. You had the talent to become a fine actor!

You have it still. You're my son—!" Our suspicion that Tyrone is exhuming the remains of an old and played-out quarrel is confirmed by Jamie's response:

> Jamie (Boredly): Let's forget me. I'm not interested in
>   the subject. Neither are you.
>   (Tyrone gives up. Jamie goes on casually.)
>   What started us on this?

It is obviously an old routine, a re-run of a performance that has been acted by Tyrone very nearly as often as his Count of Monte Cristo.

Mary Tyrone is described as "a ghost haunting the past," and so are all of O'Neill's characters in *Long Day's Journey*, all ghosts revisiting the scenes of old terror and hatreds, caught in the inescapable patterns of their pasts, bearing the "horrible burden of time." Frozen in fixed attitudes, like the inhabitants of Dante's *Inferno*, the characters express their love and their hatred in hits and withdrawals, and in defensive anger that flares up briefly before giving way to guilt, shame, and, finally, pity. The rhythm of the play leads through scenes of emotional hysteria and anger to a resolution of hopeless pity.

And yet the resolution is not factitious. It is rather a fulfillment of the dramatic rhythm itself. After witnessing and vicariously participating in so much rage and shame all aggressive and hostile emotions are worked out of the spectator. He is left too exhausted to feel anything but pity over the mutual victimizations of the Tyrone family. After such a prolonged expression of emotion what is left but pity, just as after a prolonged drunk what is left but collapse? The ultimate effect of the dramatic rhythm, then, is an emotional catharsis, a purifying purgation of hatred, rage, accusation, and resentment. As Edwin Arlington Robinson said of one of O'Neill's betters:

> He might have given Aristotle creeps,
> But surely would have given him his *katharsis*.

The catharsis here results from the expense of passion. With the expense of passion comes calm, or at least exhaustion. Or, to put it another way, the characters go through hell in order to achieve purgatory. But it is not so much the characters in O'Neill's play who achieve purgation as the playwright himself. As Gelb and Gelb's fine biography reveals, O'Neill's drama was his own long day's journey into night, a voyage back to the roots of his obsessions.

O'Neill wrote in his dedication to his wife, Carlotta, that the play was "of old sorrow, written in tears and blood." The dedication to Carlotta went deeper than the conventional literary dedication, since Carlotta provided the psychic support that made the play possible: "I meant it as a tribute to your love and tenderness which gave me the faith in love that enabled me to face my dead at last and write this play—write it with deep pity and understanding and forgiveness for *all* the four haunted Tyrones." It would be too simple, however, to say that all the play expresses is O'Neill's forgiveness of his family and himself. As Gelb and Gelb acutely note, "It is true that he pitied and understood. But the fact that he was impelled, years after their deaths, to reveal his father as a miser, his mother as a narcotics addict, his brother as an alcoholic, indicates that he could not entirely forgive. O'Neill, in his fifties, was still torn by alternating hatred and love for his family."[7] The point is that O'Neill achieved forgiveness by having the courage to resurrect and relive his past hatreds. The writing of the play was itself an intense emotional experience:

O'Neill was a spiritually, mentally, and physically tormented man during the two years it took him to write *Long Day's Journey Into Night*. He was as much tortured because it was agony to relive his painful past as because he was guilty at laying bare the secrets of that past.

"At times I thought he'd go mad," Carlotta recalled. "It was terrifying to watch his suffering."[8]

---

[7] Arthur and Barbara Gelb, *O'Neill* (New York: Delta Books, 1964), pp. 3–4.
[8] *Ibid.*, p. 836.

But the agony was functional and necessary. O'Neill was haunted by the past—the metaphor of haunted is in the dedication and the word "ghost" is a *leitmotif* in the drama—and his reliving of past agony was essentially a prolonged exorcism. To expel the phantoms of his past required a long day's journey into night, thus exemplifying the lesson that Edwin Arlington Robinson's Luke Havergal learned: "The dark will end the dark if anything."

Albee's dramatic sense revealed itself in his perception of the underlying form of exorcism in O'Neill's play and in his abstraction of the form to fit his own purposes. Albee himself told Melwyn Gussow that he started *Virginia Woolf* with the idea of a play that would have an exorcism at the end.[9] The whole play is meant to build towards the exorcism of the characters' demons. How successfully does Albee carry off his central conception of the purgation and expulsion of the rooted evils in his characters' souls? In the course of answering this question I shall bracket, though only for the moment, the interwoven question of Albee's definition of evil.

Albee's play is broken up into three acts entitled "Fun and Games," "Walpurgisnacht," and "The Exorcism." In my discussion of George's and Martha's childishness I have already partially explained the significance of "Fun and Games." "Fun and Games" is also part of the decadence theme that one critic, earlier mentioned, found so outrageous. What, after all, have George and Martha to do but play their nasty games? They are not altogether unrepresentative of one type of American, up with the fashionable ideas and the stock opinions but completely uninterested in politics and viewing all of life in terms of the sciences that bear on the private life: psychology and biology.

The one seemingly social problem that the characters talk about is the remote prospect of an attempt to enforce genetic uniformity— a world made up of exact reproductions of Nick. Even this is not a genuine social issue but rather a psychological projection of George's

[9] Gussow, in *Newsweek*, pp. 52–53.

assurances of inferiority, taking the form of fears that he is biologi-
cally unfit, a logical candidate for castration, though judging from
his relationship with Martha it would seem rather late in the day
for George to be worrying. As Martha aptly remarks, biology is
"right at the *meat* of things," and even George, who keeps reminding everyone that he is an historian, sometimes appears to be confused. He upsets Nick, for instance, by saying that history is on
Nick's side:

Nick: Unh, unh. *You've* got history on *your* side . . . I've got biology on
    mine. History, biology.
George: I know the difference.
Nick: You don't act it.

And George does not act it, continually throughout the play confusing history with biology and psychology, in keeping with the
reduction of the world to the purely private.

Forced back on personal relations such people have no inner resources with which to maintain the trying rituals of polite society.
To put the situation in literary terms, these people would be too
disengaged from social issues to interest novelists in the Zola tradition and too empty and mannerless to interest novelists in the
James tradition. For that matter, all that such persons are interested
in is themselves, and their lives are a continual psychodrama, interesting only for their momentary psychic dominance over others
—the will to power conceived in strictly private terms—or for their
humiliating defeats. Their fun and games lack order, partaking of
the chaos though not the vitality of a feast of misrule.

George and Martha's world is in violent antithesis to that of Virginia Woolf's female protagonist, Clarissa Dalloway, "the perfect
hostess." Virginia Woolf's character is the embodiment of the *esprit
de finesse*, of the faculty that finds order in life and makes fine dis-
criminations in the face of a persuasive chaos. The world of Mrs.
Dalloway, in effect, represents the opposite of George and Martha's
crude and violent play pen. George and Martha's chant of "Who's

Afraid of Virginia Woolf" is a childish defiance of the principles
of order, judgment, taste, and decency in the everyday conduct
of the private life. Nor is this obvious-enough interpretation dis-
proved by the fact that Albee first saw the phrase "Who's Afraid
of Virginia Woolf" scrawled on the blackboard of a Greenwich Village Bar.[10] Greenwich Village is itself a regressive subculture, allowing bohemians from the hinterlands to prolong their adolescence
beyond normal bounds.

That "Fun and Games" leads on to a *"Walpurgisnacht"* is not
surprising, since sexual promiscuity is a popular way to pass the
time while "waiting for the end." Since Albee uses the German
form, he was probably thinking of Goethe's *Faust*. St. Walpurgis
was an English nun who became abbess of a Bavarian convent and
whose day was May 1; however, the *Walpurgisnacht* itself is not a
celebration in honor of the saint but rather the traditional date of
the witch revels on the Brocken, atop the highest point of the Harz
mountains. The connection of the saint's name with such unsaintly
doings is probably twofold: first, the saint is a charm against the
witches; secondly, the worship of the saint was imposed on a traditional pagan ritual. But this is mere speculation. What is certain
is that in German folklore and in Goethe's *Faust* the *Walpurgisnacht*
is a wild explosion of evil forces, an utterly depraved orgy characterized partially by the young witch who offers lovely fruit to Faust
but upsets him when a scarlet mouse springs out of her mouth.

Albee's play has no Faust but Martha substitutes nicely for all
the witches, and her constant profanity, for the red mouse. She is,
after all, the *daughter* of a white mouse with red eyes. The orgies,
however, in Albee's play are not really sexual; they are orgies of
hate and humiliation. The second act is a *Walpurgisnacht* in that
the fun and games have shifted to "total war," the characters wield
their razors with complete abandon, and by the end of the act there
is blood all over the floor. Martha does her witch dance and finishes
by dragging Nick off to the bedroom.

[10] *Ibid.*

That "The Exorcism" follows *"Walpurgisnacht"* is the logic of Albee's form. The verbal violence is so extreme and so sustained that its logical result is exhaustion. An attempt to crown the verbal violence with physical violence, for instance, would have been a banal anticlimax. Even the profanity serves the formal effect of breaking through the audience's emotional resistance, battering at them to the point of ultimate exhaustion. The play by its very formal structure then demands cessation of violence, necessitates an exorcism. The audience is ready for a partial resolution of George and Martha's conflict—what else could there be? Yet it is precisely here—at the carefully prepared-for point of exorcism—that Albee's play is unconvincing.

"The Exorcism" is formally and dramatically convincing as the necessary end of a formal sequence that moves through violence to exhaustion and forgiveness, but it is entirely unconvincing in terms of plot, theme, and character. There is an immense wrench as Albee attempts to shift gears from the heightened realism of violence to the symbolic representation of exorcism. What is exorcised is not really the characters' violence and hatred but a symbolic child who apparently is meant to stand for falsehood and illusion, for the false justifications George and Martha employ to avoid a final confrontation of the void they live in. The need to abolish illusion is meaningful enough but the modern variation of the idea is, unfortunately, about on the level of George and Martha's nightmare version of "the private life." Our final guilt and shame, it is held in this post-Freudian era, are due to our refusal to banish falsehood and illusion about our psyches, to our insistence on rationalization and self-justification. Psychological honesty, the peeling off of labels to get down to the bare bone—this is the new ethic. This ethic might take its motto from Swift: "Last week I saw a woman *flay'd,* and you will hardly believe how much it altered her Person for the worse." Surely no more ridiculous version of a salvational nostrum, no sillier confusion of means with ends has ever been offered than this new and fashionable doctrine of psychological reductionism—truth defined in wholly clinical terms. Yet its main competitor in the market of revised ethics is the equally banal dogma of sexual and personal "fulfillment" vended in our popular magazines. The flayed woman competes with the mechanical playmate.

Thus part of Albee's difficulty in his ending is that he yields to the newest cliché, the latest panacea. Moreover, even if we accept Albee's ethical cliché, we find his symbol—the invented child—contrived and incredible. We can believe in all of George and Martha's games except this final one. One can only agree with Alfred Chester that the child fantasy is a red herring planted to mystify and eventually surprise the audience, a dramatic gimmick rather than a meaningful symbol.[11] The symbolism of the mass for the dead that George reads over the corpse of the child symbol is more convincing but ultimately this symbolism too is a false transcendence.

Albee cannot be blamed for attempting transcendence, for transcendence in a literary work is what differentiates the very good from the great: it is what Faulkner's novels had and Erskine Caldwell's lacked; it is one of the things that put Shakespeare and Marlowe in a different sphere from Webster and Ford. Transcendence in a literary work is the lifting up of characters and plot into a moment of spiritual judgment and illumination. The characters and their actions are "placed" by their relation to this transcendent zone and their sometime ability to briefly reach it. Moreover, transcendence is not an escape from the "real world" but a transfiguration of it.

An author's ability to attain transcendence is not, as has been often supposed, solely a question of great language. Albee has a much greater control over language than O'Neill, yet *Long Day's Journey* achieves transcendence whereas *Virginia Woolf* muffs it. Thus Edmund's monologue on the sea is completely convincing as a transcendent experience although second-rate in language and in rhythm:

[11] Chester, "Edward Albee," pp. 296–301.

Only a lazy ground swell and a slow drowsy roll of the ship. The passengers asleep and none of the view in sight. No sound of man. Black smoke pouring from the funnels behind and beneath me. Dreaming, not keeping lookout, feeling alone, and above, and apart, watching the dawn creep like a painted dream over the sky and sea which slept together. Then the moment of ecstatic freedom came. The peace, the end of the quest, the last harbor, the joy of belonging to a fulfillment beyond men's lousy, pitiful, greedy fears and hopes and dreams! And several other times in my life, when I was swimming far out, or lying alone on a beach, I have had the same experience. Became the sun, the hot sand, green seaweed anchored to a rock, swaying in the tide. Like a saint's vision of beatitude. Like the veil of things as they seem drawn back by an unseen hand. For a second you see—and seeing the secret, are the secret. For a second there is meaning! Then the hand lets the veil fall and you are alone, lost in the fog again, and you stumble on toward nowhere, for no good reason!

A second moment of transcendence comes at the end of O'Neill's play. Here the transcendence is Mary's, accomplished, ironically, through a momentary dope-induced madness and introduced sardonically by Jamie: "The Mad Scene. Enter Ophelia." As Mary, lost in the past, proceeds with her explanation of how Mother Elizabeth discouraged her from becoming a nun, she transcends any merely sentimental pathos:

I never dreamed Holy Mother would give me such advice! I was really shocked. I said, of course, I would do anything she suggested, but I know it was simply a waste of time. After I left her, I felt all mixed up, so I went to the shrine and prayed to the Blessed Virgin and found peace again because I knew she heard my prayer and would always love me and see no harm ever came to me so long as I never lost my faith in her.
    (She pauses and a look of growing uneasiness comes over her face. She passes a hand over her forehead as if brushing cobwebs from her brain—vaguely.)
That was in the winter of senior year. Then in the spring something happened to me. Yes, I remember. I fell in love with James Tyrone and was so happy for a time.

It should be noted that both these transcendent moments grow from out of the past. The transcendent writer—Proust and Tolstoy are obvious examples—sees experience as a complex relation of past and present. The nontranscendent writer, in contrast, creates only an eternal present. The difficulty with George's quotations from the Mass for the Dead is that they have no relation to any created or even implied past experience either of the character or, for that matter, of the playwright. O'Neill earned his transcendent experiences of the sea; they are part of his character's past and of his own. But when has George been a professing Catholic? George's Catholic symbolism has no real context. What might be convincing in Graham Greene, François Mauriac, or Georges Bernanos is merely unearned mystification in Albee. Moreover, Albee leaves us with an unresolved confusion over George's motive—is he trying to punish Martha or save her? When he first conceives of slaughtering their imaginary child his motive is clearly revengeful, but later, with no indication of any shift in George's character, he seems as clearly to be acting as a priestly exorcist of his and Martha's common demon of untruth. But since the child is an unconvincing symbol of untruth and illusion, bad symbolism fails to rescue inconsistent characterization.

Is then *Virginia Woolf* a failure? I think not. What Philip Roth said about *Tiny Alice* applies to *Virginia Woolf* as well: "Albee sees in human nature very much what Maupassant did, only he wants to talk about it like Plato. In this way he not only distorts his own observations, but subverts his own powers, for it is not the riddles of philosophy that bring his talent to life, but the ways of cruelty and humiliation."[12] If Albee's symbolism and pseudo-religious transcendence are unreal, his presentation of the private hell his characters live in, a hell differing from Sartre's only in that the door is always open with a welcome mat outside, is entirely real and convincing. Albee is not a symbolist but he is a brilliant comedian of

[12] Philip Roth, "The Play That Dare Not Speak Its Name," *The New York Review of Books*, IV, No. 2 (February 25, 1965), 4.

sickness, a virtuoso of humiliation and cruelty. The invective in *Virginia Woolf* has an almost medieval vigor. Thus, Martha: "If you existed I'd divorce you." And her much-quoted comment after Nick's bedroom failure: "I am the earth mother and you're all flops." George's counterattacks are less blunt but equally effective, as in his description of Martha's method of courtship: "She'd sit outside of my room, on the lawn, at night, and she'd howl and claw at the turf." George also conducts a limited war on the clichés that keep popping out of Nick and Honey. When Honey wants to powder her nose George asks Martha to direct her to the "euphemism." He nails Nick's attempt to make conversation about an abstract painting:

Nick: It's got a . . . a . . .
George: A quiet intensity?
Nick: Well, no . . . a . . .
George: Oh. (Pause.) Well, then, a certain noisy relaxed
   quality, maybe?
Nick: (Knows what George is doing, but stays grimly, coolly
   polite) No. What I meant was . . .
George: How about . . . uh . . . a quietly relaxed noisy
   intensity?

Albee's fine management of timing is evident throughout:

Martha: (After a moment's consideration) You make me puke!
George: What?
Martha: Uh . . . you make me puke!

The stage direction in Martha's first line—indicating a pause to choose the most appropriate and elegant term—and the slight hitch in her next line—as if she really needed to make a mental effort to recall her exact words—transform what might have been trite invective into cruel comedy.

In the context of this comic inferno one can justify even some obtrusive bits of symbolism, such as George's entrance with "Flores. Flores para los muertos. Flores" and his use of the second move-

ment of Beethoven's Seventh Symphony for dance music—the dance
of death, needless to say. Here, in fact, in the very devilishness of
his characters Albee approaches the transcendence he failed to
achieve in his Catholic symbolism. Or, to put it more accurately, he
approaches what Saul Bellow in his latest novel sardonically termed
"transcendence downward" or "trans-descendence."[13] Thus George
and Martha are clearly superior to Nick and Honey because whereas
George and Martha are awful, Nick and Honey are merely null.
Albee values demons over dullards, as it were. And then it should
be remembered that Nick and Honey are not less neurotic than
George and Martha, only quieter. George and Martha's self-drama-
tization gives them a superior reality and even gives their lives a
perverse form. All they have is their illness but at least they assert
imagination by converting illness into drama and humiliation into
a game. I do not agree with Sartre that this type of trans-descendence
is a legitimate title to sanctification—as Sartre holds in the case of
Genet—nor should it be forgotten that sick drama was a genre not
of theatre but of world politics Hitler-style in the thirties and forties,
played with mountains of corpses for checkers. Nevertheless, surely
Nick reflects the audience response in his reluctant admiration of
George and Martha:

> George: It isn't the prettiest spectacle . . . seeing a couple of middle-
> aged types hacking away at each other, all red in the face and winded,
> missing half the time.
> Nick: Oh, you two don't miss . . . you two are pretty good. Impressive.
> George: And impressive things impress you, don't they? You're . . .
> easily impressed . . . sort of a . . . pragmatic idealism.
> Nick: (A tight smile) No, it's that sometimes I can admire things that
> I don't admire. Now, flagellation isn't my idea of good times . . .
> George: . . . but you can admire a good flagellator . . . a real pro.

Moreover, again in the transdescendent style, George and Martha
have a genuine relationship, a symbiotic dependence on each other's

---

[13] Saul Bellow, *Herzog* (New York: Viking, 1964), pp. 163, 176.

cruelty and humiliations. One can only conjecture what George and Martha would be like if they should straighten out, as Albee hints at the end they may, what with the imaginary child dead and a new fear of Virginia Woolf. Their humanity and their conflict seem inseparable. But odd as it sounds, they have a happier marriage than Nick and Honey. Honey could never, with any sincerity, deliver a tribute to Nick like Martha's to George: "There is only one man in my life who has ever . . . made me happy." Almost, in their sad, cruel comedy they achieve some measure of transcendence after all:

George who is out there somewhere in the dark . . . George who is good to me, and whom I revile; who understands me, and whom I push off; who can make me laugh, and I choke it back in my throat; who can hold me at night, so that it's warm, and whom I will bite so there's blood; who keeps learning the games we play as quickly as I can change the rules; who can make me happy and I do not wish to be happy, and yes I do wish to be happy. George and Martha: sad, sad, sad.

Hubris, Health, and Holiness: The Despair of J. F. Powers

Robert G. Twombly

The preceding papers have dealt so relentlessly with the theme of "despair" that I wonder if anyone will really have the patience to put up with a final paper that goes so far as to have the dread word part of its title. My subtitle, "The Despair of J. F. Powers," gives my thesis away a little prematurely; and if the thing were possible, I should ask you therefore to forget that subtitle for the time being, and consider Powers in the way the majority of his critics have considered him up to now. His reviewers seem to feel almost to a man that his is a thoroughly virile and healthy outlook. He has a sharp satiric tongue for the hypocrite and a forthright compassion for the victim of hypocrisy. And both satire and compassion imply, one would suppose, a firm sense of the objective difference between good and bad, virtues and faults, the genuine and the sham. He belongs to our new generation of moralists, prepared to judge a human act or human motive on its intrinsic merits, against standards of honesty and rationality and charity that are taken to be objective and absolute.

Like Mary McCarthy, or John Cheever, Powers owes much of his popularity to his ability to write anecdotal satire, stories in which the hypocrisy that is exposed is confined within the limits of a single incident, and confined therefore to one time, one place, and often to one person. This ability of Powers' might be explained as a response to the demands of his favorite publisher, *The New Yorker*, a magazine that likes its satires safely muzzled and incapable of biting more than one class or ethnic group at a time. In any case, whatever the cause may be, the result of Powers' growing tendency toward writing anecdotal satire has been for him to seem, as a moralist, less interested in evil, more interested in sins; less interested in Man's fallen state, more interested in particular instances of pride and hypocrisy. Powers has not always leaned toward the particular and individual in this way, as a glance at an early story, such as "Renner," will reveal. But his popularity still rests on his wit in unmasking private sins. His satire within this area can be cutting. The ripest targets, of course, are priests, the very mention of whose ecclesiastical rank is for Powers an invitation to measure the man against the office, his lusts against his vows.

Monsignor (he is known only by that increasingly ironic epithet), in the story entitled "The Forks," takes full advantage of the fact that he is not, strictly speaking, bound to poverty or obedience. Chastity of course is another matter. But if a vow can suppress carnality according to the letter of the law, it cannot so easily enforce the spirit of the law. There are intricate sublimations for even a simple man's lusts:

> Monsignor stopped in admiration a few feet from the car—her. He was as helpless before her beauty as a boy with a birthday bicycle. He could not leave her alone. He had her out every morning and afternoon and evening. He was indiscriminate about picking people up for a ride in her. He kept her on a special diet—only the best of gas and oil and grease, with daily rubdowns. He would run her only on the smoothest roads and at so many miles an hour. That was to have stopped at the first five hundred, but only now, nearing the thousand mark, was he able to bring himself to increase her speed, and it seemed to hurt him more than it did her.
>
> Now he was walking around behind her to inspect the tires. Apparently O.K. He gave the left rear fender an amorous chuck and eased into the front seat. Then they drove off, the car and he, to see the world, to explore each other further on the honeymoon.[1]

The satire guides our attention simply and straightforwardly to the particular Deadly Sin indulged, or the particular Contrary Virtue violated. Sometimes the ironic narrator even goes so far as explicitly to name it for us:

---

[1] J. F. Powers, *The Prince of Darkness and Other Stories* (New York: Doubleday and Company, 1958), p. 92.

The car, black, beautiful, fierce with chromium, was quiet as Monsignor dismounted, knowing her master. Monsignor went around to the rear, felt a tire, and probed a nasty cinder in the tread.

"Look at that," he said, removing the cinder.

Father Eudex thought he saw the car lift a hoof, gaze around, and thank Monsignor with her headlights.

Monsignor proceeded at a precise pace to the back door of the rectory. There he held the screen open momentarily, as if remembering something or reluctant to enter before himself—such was his humility—[2]

The precision and directedness of this kind of satire, a combination of the small, self-enclosed incident, with its own straight-faced, motive-assigning, descriptive comment, reaches a high point in "The Prince of Darkness," a story in which the priest-protagonist in essence commits, in the course of one day and with the finesse of his own golf game or his own fast driving, each one of the Seven Deadly Sins. The story is a neat, but subtly arranged catalogue of vices. The protagonist is himself the Prince of Darkness, for his legal name is Ernest Burner, a name which his Archbishop is unable to find on any list of saints. Near the end the Archbishop himself appropriately expresses, to the ever-politic Burner, the thought that could well stand for the author's own *apparent* outlook in these short, anecdotal satires:

"We look hard to the right and left, Father. It is rather to the center, I think, we should look—to ourselves, the devil in us."

Father Burner knew the cue for humility when he heard it. "Yes, Your Excellency."[3]

Perhaps there is only the faintest of ominous notes in the fact that the earnest burner is too intent on his own prudential humility to hear the Archbishop's sound, healthy, moral advice. And perhaps at this point it will never enter the reader's head to question whether the author is really as optimistic a moral therapist as the Archbishop.

[2] *Ibid.*, pp. 95–96.
[3] *Ibid.*, p. 191.

It is, I think, with expectations engendered by such stories as this that most readers have approached Powers' novel, *Morte d'Urban*. The reviewers of the book, for instance, consistently give a picture of Powers in which they have armed him with all the paraphernalia of the topical satirist; and in this case that means intimate and detailed perceptions of what the Catholic hierarchy is "really like." At the outset, the task implicitly or explicitly assigned Powers is that, in exposing the weaknesses and absurdities in the personality of a priest, the George Babbitt of American Catholicism, the book must both chastise those weaknesses and absurdities and, like Lewis' book, ultimately become an apologia for the man and the life that it criticizes. Only one critic, to my knowledge, has had sense enough to perceive in *Morte d'Urban* a note of bitterness not found in Lewis' *Babbitt*. And even that critic reveals his contrary expectations by expressing shocked surprise at the book's antiecclesiasticism. The other critics confidently go on looking for the Powers stance, and listening for the Powers style, to which we have become accustomed in the wittier short stories.

There is, of course, an excuse for finding *Morte d'Urban* a vigorous and confident affirmation, albeit indirect, of what Powers and other serious Catholics feel their Church hierarchy ought to be like, and what motives ought to guide its members. Late in the book, as Father Urban Roche, the protagonist, is reciting the ritual wherein he is to become Provincial of the Order of Saint Clement, the reader may suppose that he has come upon precisely that expression of the moral norm that anchors the satiric point of view within the positive, the healthy, the creative affections:

What are the three corners of truth?
Reason, by which we examine ourselves. Love, by which we sympathize with others. Purity, by which we are lifted to invisible heights.[4]

---

[4] J. F. Powers, *Morte d'Urban* (New York: Popular Library, 1963), p. 263. Future references to this novel will appear in my text, in the form of page numbers within parentheses.

On earlier pages Urban Roche has been found wanting on two of the three counts. Now things may have changed. The prescriptive character of this rule, and its aphoristic form, are reminiscent of Father Urban's own somewhat slick sermons. Unlike the sermons, though, the ritual is produced in its entirety, unaccompanied by any narrative whatever, and so may be understood wholly seriously, our sense of its intended meaning unsullied by any implication of its speaker's hypocrisy. Father Urban, here at the end of the novel, is quite free of the taint of pride. And from the disappearance of the ironic narrator some reviewers infer that the spirit of moral criticism has come to rest.

This fading out of the ironic narrator at the end, interestingly, is the only way in which Powers can convey a change in attitude within his central character. From the first page of the novel the central point of view has been Father Urban's. In this, above all, the style of the novel differs crucially from the style of the short stories. Powers has developed more and more highly the kind of tonal subtlety in narrative that allows Urban, for instance, to look in all ways shallow and foolish, but without either Urban's becoming aware of it, or the narrator's abandoning Urban's point of view. At the climax of a mission he is conducting, Urban is made to parody, with a single, brief, inserted line of direct address, his own homey, familiar sermon style. Then, half a dozen lines later, the subtlest raising of the reader's expectations, as Urban gazes upward as if for a vision, ends in the nearly imperceptible burlesque of that vision:

"Do these things, and the gentle rain of God's loving mercy will fall upon you and yours! Now and for all time! *Now! Forever! If!*"

Forty-five minutes earlier, Father Urban had begun with those three little words, treating them, he said, as an etymologist might—"Now don't let *that* scare you, it only means wordsmith"—and, having made no great demands on the three little words then, he'd left them, had entirely forgotten them, so it must have seemed to the congregation, but he hadn't. In the end, he'd come back to them, and those three little words, two shouted and one whispered, had gone off like fireworks, like two bombs and a pinwheel. And thus another mission had ended—almost.

Still in the pulpit, Father Urban, eloquent in silence, stared out over the heads of the congregation and saw what nobody else in the old church could see so well, the clock in the choir loft, which said eight-forty. Making the sign of the cross, which rippled through the congregation, he turned and, for a moment, was invisible to the people. When he next appeared to them, he was down on their level, leaving the pulpit, walking, kneeling before them—for this purpose a *prie-dieu* had been placed in a central position in the sanctuary. (136)

There is no satire here strong enough to make Father Urban seem another Burner. In fact the irony in the style of this book is so consistently low-key that it is hard to find passages whose tone will survive this kind of lifting out of context. Even in context it is hard now to pin down a particular sin in Father Urban; for it is rather his impeccability itself that is disturbing. The satire, for all its subtlety, runs deep; for the rigid consistency in seeing things ostensibly from Urban's point of view, combined with the recurring double-take produced by a regular sequence of small absurdities (like the clock, or the *prie-dieu*), produces a constant sense of what we are often told is going on: namely, that Urban is watching himself unceasingly in the mirrors of his own mind, watching himself critically, but without humor. This, by the way, is his sin, if he has one. And so long as the narrator is present, our sense of Urban's self-detachment persists, together with our sense that this self-detachment makes him a kind of hypocrite.

Urban is a keen critic, a keen self-critic, but a thoroughly amoral one. From the ethical standpoint this is eventually a form of pride. From any other standpoint, this most persistent quality in Urban simply marks him as a compulsive disciple of Stephen Potter. And when Powers allows simpler and more saintly men to be better gamesmen than Father Urban we experience a curious multiple fracture between our moral, and our intellectual and aesthetic sympathies. For instance, we must agree with Urban that the two fellow priests, with whom he is cooped up for Advent, are beyond endurance. They have neither taste nor tact. They wrestle with the most trivial question as grimly as if it had been the doctrine of the Fall. Urban picks an evening-long fight with one of them, Wilf, over the fact that Wilf has stolen the Christ-child from Urban's own electrified, revolving crêche, and hidden it, since it is not yet Christmas Eve. The argument is finally neutralized, but not before the scene has come to resemble Browning's Spanish Cloister:

Wilf went over to the tree, knelt, and disconnected the crib, stopping the animals and shepherds in their tracks. But then, to Father Urban's surprise, Wilf reached up into the branches of the tree and brought out the bambino and put it back where it belonged—and thus, though it might seem all was well now, they arrived at the moment Father Urban had been waiting for. He let it pass, however.

"Thanks," he'd been going to say at that moment. "Thanks," as he might have said it, would have been quite enough for him. But he had denied himself that pleasure, and if Wilf would just leave it at that, so would he. Wasn't this the *true* meaning of Christmas? Joy to the world and peace to men of *good* will. It was hard, though—oh, very hard—to see someone having it both ways.

Wilf, having plugged in the crib, returned to his rocker. He picked up the paper, and then, boldly meeting Father Urban's gaze, he said: "Just shows how wrong we can be sometimes."

We! As if Father Urban had been wrong about anything! He glared at Jack, and stared him down, his eyes following Jack's down to the checkerboard—where he saw a surprising opportunity. He was not forgetting Wilf, but he would deal with Jack first. With his only king, Father Urban jumped this way and that, taking a dreadful toll of Jack's black men.

"Why didn't *I* see that?" said Jack. Something in his tone, and, on second thought, the easiness of the conquest on the board, suggested to Father Urban that Jack had indeed seen it, had planned it, had offered himself and his black men for sacrifice. Thereupon, though he didn't like what Jack had done, the desire to deal with Wilf died in Father Urban. (88–89)

Father Urban is as fully aware as we are of the complexity of a situation; so much so that he is habitually, and accurately, totting-up his one-upmanship score. It is true that Urban does not imme-diately appreciate the vanity of scorekeeping. Nor is he prepared to pass *moral* judgment on the vanities he does perceive. But in all other respects he is, through the controlled perspective of the inter-vening narrator, the reader's critical equal.

In other words, the result of Powers' delicate control of point of view is that the folly we are laughing at in this satire is not the folly of obtuseness, but the folly of subtlety, of watching others and watching the self in a manner too intricate to admit direct, simple, useful, moral judgments. The reviewers who compare Urban and Babbitt have the satiric thrust precisely backwards. As a moralist Powers is here condemning not a man's sins, but a man's incapacity for either virtue or sin. Urban is neither hot nor cold. And this bal-ance, this deadly neutrality of the sensibility that is merely self-aware, and merely critical, is the product of a correlative balance, finely critical, in the narrative voice. The two become linked in-separably:

> *No, but* and *Yes, but* and *On the other hand* and *Much as I agree with you*, and *Apart from that* and *Far be it from me*—Father Urban, it seemed, was always trying to present the other side, the balanced view. This kept him busy, for Monsignor Renton talked like a drunken curate. One moment it was "God is not mocked" or "Christ, and Christ cruci-fied," and the next moment it was "Your ass is out." (119)

The result is that when, at the end of the book, Powers must convey a change in Father Urban, a falling-away of his critical sense, and an end to his pursuit of one-upmanship, the only way he can do this is by abandoning the narrative voice altogether. For the last six pages of what amounts to the last chapter (not counting a fiercely ironic epilogue, which we will get to presently), the writing is either direct stage dialogue, straight reproduction of ritual (in parallel Latin-English columns), or, when narrative is unavoidable, a rigorously uncolored narration, all in italics to avoid any confusion with the narrative presence of the rest of the book.

It is, as I said, in response to this stylistic and typographic change that Powers' reviewers have assumed that the satire's moral norm lies within Powers' final fictitious ritualization of love, reason, and purity. They have not cared to notice, at least consciously, the real and inescapable implication of ritual when it is mere ritual. (And Powers leaves no doubt that the reciting of "Regula S. Clementis necnon Rituale Ordinis Ejus" is the merest formality.) If ritual represents the very body of a vital impulse, it represents only the husk of a dead one. And there is reason, more than is found in just the book's title, for pronouncing Father Urban Roche at this point stone dead. But we will return to this momentarily.

Those who seek in the last chapter the satirist's unsatirical affirmation of belief, must describe the change that has taken place in Urban as a change for the better, and account for that change in terms of some seriously meaningful incident within the action. (It is one of the misdirected criticisms of the book that there is no such clearly serious incident. This is precisely correct.) Father Urban is the self-possessed, eloquent, socially adept "road man" for the otherwise dour, dusty, and pious Order of St. Clement. For reasons known only to God (who is not consulted) he finds himself taken off the road and assigned to the bedraggled crew that is painting and plastering an old and unpleasant country house, for the use of retreatants. Henceforward, by slow and frustrated degrees, involving the careful manipulation of a few clergy, women, and millionaires, Urban manages to transform both the country estate and his own job into something more to his liking. In particular, he surrounds the ascetic old religious house with a good golf course, and acquires for his own use, on preaching trips, the fast sports car of a benefactress. At this point, two events give sudden new shape to the action.

Fearing the growing influence of the order, and covetous of the country house it maintains, the local Bishop attempts an act of simple gamesmanship that will be a first step toward taking over the estate. He challenges Father Urban at golf; and wisely provides himself with a young champion who is almost Urban's match. Urban hurries back to defend what has become in effect his own kingdom; and wins, not by beating the Bishop or his assistant, but by the far more effective (albeit unintended) ploy of being suddenly knocked unconscious and nearly killed by a wild shot of the Bishop's. The Order has retained its house; and Urban has acquired, perhaps like Arthur at the hands of Mordred, a head wound that may be seen as at least figuratively mortal.

Shortly hereafter, and still purely for the good of the order, Urban accompanies the Clementines' most prodigal benefactor on a fishing trip. Urban is fascinated by the man, who is emotionally and intellectually a three-year-old, and who therefore has precisely that degree of invulnerability that makes him the unbeatable gamesman. But it also makes him cruel, boorish, and in the long run a very poor sport; and Father Urban wakes up to these faults one by one, but moments too late for the good of his own health. Billy, the millionaire, from the boat in which they are fishing, grabs the antlers of a swimming deer; and Father Urban for a moment tries to play along with this as compliantly as he has always played along with everything else:

> Then he realized that Billy was trying to drown the deer.
> There was power in the deer's neck, but there was no foundation for it. When Billy braced his elbows on the gunwale, he was able to turn the deer by its antlers. When he got the animal squared away from the boat, he pressed down. Father Urban saw the deer's eyes—big black bubbles—watching him, he thought, and he looked away. He *heard* bubbles then, and heard the antlers rubbing against the boat. He was feeling strongly what he'd felt only slightly on several occasions in the last three days. He was feeling cheap. (231)

For the first time in his life the urbane Father is shocked enough at himself to take the moral initiative. He "guns" the outboard, toppling Billy out of the boat and saving the deer; and saving also, as Urban thinks complacently to himself, the soul of this sadistic, six-foot child. But Father Urban's customary way of winning souls is with graciousness and studied self-effacement. And this is the tactic he employs as Billy climbs aboard:

> "I'm sorry, but I had to do it," Father Urban said. He started to re-move his sweater, meaning to give it to Billy.
>
> Billy indicated that he didn't want the sweater, and then that he wished to run the motor.
>
> Father Urban got the impression that Billy wasn't talking to him yet—that the situation was still dangerous, but that Billy was making a tremendous effort to control himself. . . . They were in for a rough ride, Father Urban was thinking, when Billy pushed him overboard.
>
> Father Urban, an able swimmer, came smiling to the surface, return-ing good for evil. He stopped this, though, when Billy . . . reeling in [his line], drove off without him. (232)

Urban, it seems, has for the first two times in his life lost con-trol of the situation, actually suffered physically, and, still more ironically, won and lost his biggest point scores in each case with a swift violence that completely routs both his wits and his urbanity. He has by mischance saved the golf course and retreat house from the hands of the enemy; but he has, also by mischance, lost the Order's readiest source of income; and in fact even the victory over the Bishop is only temporary. The denouement is at hand. And it is reasonable to expect a change, even a new humility, in Urban. The story is rapidly taking on elements of the pastoral, and of the romance. Indeed, even the symbols are supplied. For Arthur's death-wound bestowed a kind of sanctity, and a concomitant im-mortality. And Christian baptism is rebirth, and signals the be-ginning of a new kind of existence. And besides, when next we see Urban, he has exchanged black garb for white (his other clothes being wet), has spent an hour at a familiar bus station without being recognized by anyone, and is just being picked up by a woman in a white convertible (who an hour later, to round out the symbolism, transports him across the water to her lonely castle). What readers who take this kind of thing seriously fail to notice is that Father Urban, far from exhibiting a change of anything more than clothes, is still pursuing wholeheartedly the winning game. His knowledge of good cars serves him well. The woman greets him tentatively; then, "He smiled back, and, trusting his memory of the car, he took a chance: 'Mrs. Hopwood?' "

Urban is in fact unregenerate, and the symbols, as well as the title of the book, are simply and consistently ironic. They are as arbitrary and artificial as Urban's motorized Christmas crêche; and as comfortably meaningless as the clock at the top of the church, that only Urban can see. The more we feel tempted to hunt down Arthurian and Christian symbols (and reviewers have come to grief doing this), the more we see the measure by which Urban Roche falls short of either the Holy or the chivalric ideal. If he is a knight in quest of the Grail, the affair is as much a burlesque of that myth as is the Clementines' first, expurgated, paperback, children's romance, "Sir Launcelot and the Catholic Knights of the Round Table." If Arthur's knights were unworthy of the Grail, Urban is simply unworthy of the romantic comparison with them. By far the most significant transformation in Urban is a secret and bacteriological one. As the narrator points out, his shoes and socks are still wet; and as we subsequently discover, he is soon to be in an oxygen tent with pneumonia.

But before this comes about there occurs the most significant incident in the book. For the two indignities suffered so far are direct preparation for a third, which follows hard upon the second and includes the severest test of Father Urban's moral strength. What is most important about his third blow to Urban's composure, though, is that it fuses, repeats precisely, and effectively burlesques the heroic wound and immersion baptism of the earlier two. Exaggeration and repetition will upset the semantic economy of any symbol. Double a somewhat ironic symbol, with altered circumstances, and you have doubled the perspective on that symbol, and redoubled the irony. This is precisely what Urban's mind habitually does, in his constant reassessment of every social situation. Powers is about to poke complicated fun at Urban's pretense of being straightforward, honest, and modern.

Mrs. Hopwood, soon known as Sally, conveys Father Urban to her private castle in the middle of her own lake, on the hint to him that her husband will be there. Instead of a husband, there is an open fire on a large stone hearth, a bear skin on the floor, a swan-shaped bed of woven willow, thirty-year-old whiskey, and no light but the firelight. After a while, Sally comes to the point with dextrous aim, a point which Father Urban has always been coming to, but never been simple-spirited enough to grasp:

> "Has it occurred to you that people might be disappointed by you and your reasons, and even more by you?"
>
> "I'm not sure I know what you mean," said Father Urban.
>
> "I mean you're an operator—a trained operator like Mrs. Leeson, and an operator in your heart—and I don't think you have a friend in the world."
>
> Father Urban smiled. "Now you've gone too far."
>
> "Name *one*." (242)

Sally herself is prepared to name, and to be one.

There are, as we noticed in an earlier Powers story, a variety of sexual sublimations whereby a man may reward his physical abstinence with a rich harvest of imaginings. The Grail quest is one culturally significant example of this; and the resulting quasi-religious chivalric code has been a pattern of noble endeavor since the death of the original Arthur. Amid the skins of wild animals, and confronted with a woman in a skin of her own, Father Urban's twentieth-century sublimation, though, is a vision of automated, air-conditioned bliss that falls woefully short of anything noble, or quasi-religious, or anything like a code:

> . . . A spacious office on Michigan Avenue, high up, with a view of the lake, walnut panelling, Persian carpets, furnished with gifts from potentates and dictators of the better sort, a tree at Christmas, efficient

rosy-cheeked girls in white-collared dark dresses, Irish girls hired for the purity of their vocables, and himself hardly ever there. He would have helped the girls with their grave personal problems, and they would be loyal to him and his firm forever, and never marry, and he would have put the crippled son of one of the elevator operators through school. . . . Until his marriage, he'd played around a lot, but he'd never touched waitresses, stewardesses, receptionists, the wives or mistresses of his friends, or anybody who worked for him in the office, or in the home office, or in any of his other offices throughout the world. . . . Always partial to mature women, he'd married a widow. Lovely woman. Not beef and pork but woman. Her throat not as full as it had been, perhaps, but otherwise she was as good as new, nose and mouth finely drawn, arabesque lines, eyes dark, hair plentiful, tufty (as with some birds), and mahogany, light for mahogany, expressive hands, holding whatever they held lightly . . . lovely woman whose first marriage, if you could call it that, hadn't clicked. (242–243)

Urban is watching Sally, it seems, with the same depth of appreciation he bestows on the fine whiskey.

But as Sally's clothes come off in earnest, in preparation for a swim, Urban's back is discreetly turned on her, and on the reality of the world to which he has been called to minister. He can think only of the social awkwardness of trying to make a grown woman put her clothes back on. And besides, she is a "lovely woman. No doubt of it." Sally, though, has a keen sense of reality, and of what she has been prepared to renounce for its sake. Consequently, when she removes her last stitch, a shoe, and hurls it full force at Urban's turned head, the deepening of his wound is her pedestrian blow, struck with ironically just aim, against the very source of his complicated hypocrisy.

As Urban nurses his something-less-than-noble injury, he hears Sally dive into the dark water. A moment later he is roused for the first time all evening from complacency into honest, unpremeditated response: He hears the motor start and the boat move away, leaving him stranded, appropriately, on the fairy-tale island. It is at this point that Urban's second baptism is forced upon him; and if the first baptism failed to make clear its own meaning, this one succeeds very well. Far from granting him rebirth, the water simply compounds the indignity, and the fever Urban is about to suffer. Halfway back to reality, in the middle of the lake, Urban fears a cramp and relinquishes grudgingly what Sally had relinquished willingly, his shoes. Yet, lest we imagine Urban, barefoot, as an archetypal pilgrim on his way back to the arms of his Order, Powers allows his hero prudentially to retain his socks. And the high-point of the antisymbolism, and of Urban's indignity, comes when, on surreptitiously retrieving his overnight bag from Sally's car, he finds that he has lost his clerical collar. Sally it seems has removed it, and has taken this means of showing her opinion of what he is, or is not. His priestliness, like his manliness, is "all wet."

A symbol hardly outlasts its inception. Never is the symmetry of a symbolic act allowed to prevail over the requirements of human comfort or social propriety. Nor does propriety or comfort ever prevail for very long against the peevishness of men and women, priests and bishops, who have made fools of each other. The dignity of Father Urban is reduced to a shambles, along with all the myths of romantic or pastoral ideality. He takes to his bed unaware of how swiftly his own glamor, and the glamor of the Order, is about to dissolve. The crumbling process underway in the action is a precise magnification of the crumbling process constantly afflicting the self-image that gamesman Urban has *always* been so busy patching and piecing together. Self-detachment, for the sake of one's point score, reveals too many self-delusions and mere sublimations; and eventually destroys both sympathy and purity, if not reason as well. Father Urban's reward for all he has done, for all he has thought he has done, and for all he has thought he has abstained from doing, is the total crumbling of his consciousness. He falls into a coma that lasts a week.

When he comes to, he finds himself elected Provincial of the Order of St. Clement. But it is the end of the novel, and Powers wraps up the irony with swift efficiency. The Order, after long years, have decided to enter the twentieth century by publishing *Sir Launcelot and the Catholic Knights of the Round Table*, by putting back on the air "Father Clem Answers Your Questions" (between "Civil Service News" and the "Transylvanian Hour"), and by putting Father Urban in charge of all. But Father Urban, the twentieth-century "operator," has a wound too deep to heal. In part it is indeed his head wound, which causes him with growing frequency and seriousness to stop functioning. But in larger part it is something worse, indicated as I said before by the disappearance of the narrative voice, and indicated as well, ironically, in the closing lines of the ritual: "Si contigerit (quod Deus avertat) aliquem de nostris fratribus, non in corpore, sed in anima mori; . . .": "If it should happen (which God forbid) that any of our brethren should die, not in body but in soul, so long as he is among us I will besiege the Saviour, both with my own prayers, whatever a sinner can avail, and with those of the brethren." Father Urban, not in body but in soul, is dead. The epilogue briefly sketches the pathos of this. But more importantly it indicates the parallel fate of the Clementines:

About these things, and others, he had little to say, but reading the speeches of Winston Churchill, and coming to "I have not become the King's first minister in order to preside over the liquidation of the British Empire," he thought, "No, nor did Mr. (as he was then) Attlee consider himself so called, but such was his fate."

The final culprit in this book is neither a man nor a sin. On the contrary, it is the futility of moral endeavor in a world in which the only virtues are triviality and folly, and the only sins are prudence, tact, and worldly success.

I think this novel is more profoundly funny (if I can use such an expression) as well as more profoundly discouraging than any of the short stories. Nevertheless, at the risk of implying too facile and anecdotal an irony for *Morte d'Urban*, I would sharpen our view of its final dry hopelessness by comparing its apparent outlook with that of some of the short stories. One of them, "The Devil Was a Joker," deals specifically, but tangentially with the Clementines, and with the impact which that Order's clerical imagination has upon the world. Its pamphlets, under the name of Father Clem,

tackled life's problems through numberless Joans, Jeans, Bobs, and Bills, clear-thinking college kids who, coached from the wings by jolly nuns and priests, invariably got the best of the arguments they had with the poor devils they were always meeting—atheists, euthanasianists, and the like.[5]

Myles, an ardent and flawless young man who has been dismissed from seminary for no discoverable reason whatsoever (though perhaps he is a bit too holy), takes a job as assistant to a salesman distributing Father Clem's pamphlets to the world. The job is spiritually meaningless. Mac, the salesman, also deals in pornographic matchbooks, decks of playing cards showing the lives of the saints, and a mechanical plastic rosary that attaches to the wheel of a car. He is the Devil and the Joker, a wild card in the world of small commerce. And he is as subtle as Screwtape in the temptations he offers, none of which were ever dreamed of by the seraphic hayseed, Father Clem. But the contest between Good and Evil, between Myles and Mac, takes place in a world far removed from the ever gullible and naïve Church, which seems forever to have excluded Myles from its hierarchy and good sense from its pamphlets. Good tolerates Evil, Myles puts up with Mac, only for the sake of eventually finding an opening back into the Church. This he never does, and the allegory ends with Myles, who has resisted the most subtle temptation of all, standing penniless on a streetcorner, watching Mac's car "slither" out of sight with two clergymen inside, with no prospect whatever but to hitchhike back the way he has come in the hope (utterly vain) of persuading the meanest bishop of all to take him in. The allegory is brief and clever. But it is still the end of the road for Myles. And the irony only requires attenuation to become a serious moral hopelessness.

[5] J. F. Powers, *The Presence of Grace* (New York: Athenaeum, 1962), p. 63.

Powers is not consistently cynical. But the remarkable thing is that with one exception the only modern saints whose possibility he is willing to admit are Negroes and Jews, men whose lives and whose minds and whose freedom have been so severely circumscribed (at least as Powers pictures them) that they have never had a chance to enter the Twentieth Century world of refined hypocrisy; prudence, tact, and worldly success. Powers' overstrained sanctification of a lynched Negro ("The Eye") is the most powerful, and hence the worst, example of the sentimentalism, or even pastoralism, that obscures a writer's vision of the harsher truth he really knows. Wiser writers, discussed in this same series, have shown that violence, death, and blind terror do not make a man holy. Neither is ignorance the same as Christlike simplicity. Powers knows this well enough. But the very fact that he must resort to these false equations is evidence of the length to which he must go to find a protagonist he can pity.

The one exception in Powers' hagiology of oppressed and martyred men is the priest-protagonist of Powers' only truly moving story, "Lions, Hearts, and Leaping Does." Father Didymus is an old man who has watched himself kill one affection after another, ostensibly for his religion, but actually (as he knows too well) through nothing better than the disease of alienation that afflicts ironic and cynical men. He let his brother die unvisited, and knows now that the reason was not an attachment to a higher love, but simply the cynic's acquired detachment from all loves of any kind. For pleasure, he reads the Protestant John Bale's sixteenth-century attack on all the Popes. For amusement, he expurgates the book and toys with the idea of the danger to Brother Titus' faith in allowing him to read the omitted entries. He is a thoroughly delightful man, sly, self-perceptive, and deeply troubled. He has better control of himself than Urban, and the spiritual danger is correspondingly greater too. His perceptions are forever doubling and redoubling in ironic complexity; and so when he finds that he is very ill and

probably going to die, he does not know what to do with his mind
and will. If he asks in prayer for health, he knows that this would
be a kind of hypocrisy, for he feels the illness deserved. If he asks
that the disease become a spiritual trial, he knows that this would
be presumption, for he feels himself too unsaintly for a spiritual
trial. Eventually he asks for the simplicity of mind and heart to
wish himself well. As I read it, he is asking that he be cured of his
critical self-detachment, his ironic spirit. And this, remarkably, is
the only fully honest prayer that can be made by the man whose
conscience is forever redoubling and showing itself its own ulterior
selfish motives at every turn. His irony becomes his disease, and
vice versa; and Powers has given us a glimpse of perhaps the only
serious possible way of escaping Urban Roche's self-perpetuating
hypocrisy, short of receiving a head wound.

As for Powers' view of the world in general, and of the possibility
of Good actually happening in it, this can perhaps be clarified by a
return to the story we started with, "The Forks." It is clear that
little spiritual good will ever come to the souls of men from the
direction of Monsignor. Our sympathies are on the side of Monsignor's assistant, and so are our hopes, for his name is Eudex; and he
is obviously in the world to represent the Good. He helps the janitor
hoe the garden; he gives his overshoes to freezing pickets. Monsignor thinks that he is very nearly a Communist; he advises him to
shave his armpits and behave more like a representative of the
Church. Father Eudex is gradually forced, in his own benign way,
to defy authority:

> In the dining room Father Eudex sat down at the table and said
> grace. He helped himself to a chop, creamed new potatoes, pickled beets,
> jelly, and bread. He liked jelly. Monsignor passed the butter.
> "That's supposed to be a tutti-frutti salad," Monsignor said, grimac-
> ing at his. "But she used green olives."
> Father Eudex said nothing.
> "I said she used green olives."

"I like green olives all right."
"*I* like green olives, but *not* in tutti-frutti salad."
Father Eudex replied by eating a green olive.[6]

Has Father Eudex compromised something of his own goodness? Has this reader of the *Catholic Worker*, this anti-Capitalist, this Subversive, been reduced to subversion for its own peevish sake? Father Eudex, together with each of the priests in the diocese, has received a large check from a company not known for good labor practices. And his final, morally triumphant act of defiance against this kind of pay-off in particular, and against the world in general, brings with it some doubts as to the efficacy, and even the *good*, of resisting the world:

Father Eudex walked into the bathroom. He took the Rival check from his pocket. He tore it into little squares. He let them flutter into the toilet. He pulled the chain—hard.

He went to his room and stood looking out the window at nothing. He could hear the others already giving an account of their stewardship, but could not judge them. I bought baseball uniforms for the school. I bought the nuns a new washing machine. I purchased a Mass kit for a Chinese missionary. I bought a set of matched irons. Mine helped pay for keeping my mother in a rest home upstate. I gave mine to the poor.

And you, Father?[7]

The good man is tripped up by his own goodness. The scrupulous conscience comes under this-worldly judgment and is found to be irrelevant, silly, and presumptuous. To each according to his deserts. But as the moral economy of *this* world goes its practical way, the reward of the Good Man is that he is left holding the toilet chain over the last, morally tainted, and disappearing scraps of decent opportunity the world still offers.

[6] Powers, *The Prince of Darkness*, p. 96.
[7] *Ibid.*, pp. 103–104.

INDEX